# Home of 1,000 Hits

## HISTORIC RCA STUDIO B

Historic RCA
# STUDIO B
NASHVILLE

™

Studio B, c. 1962.

**Country Music Foundation Press**
222 Fifth Avenue South • Nashville, Tennessee 37203

978-0-915608-27-0

Produced by the staff of the Country Music Hall of Fame and Museum

Writer: John W. Rumble    Editor: Jay Orr    Designer: Margaret Pesek

The artifacts, documents, and photographs contained in this book come from the
collection of the Country Music Hall of Fame® and Museum unless otherwise noted.

This 1958 brochure features Steve Sholes,
who was responsible for signing Elvis Presley to RCA.
*Courtesy of Merle Atkins Russell
and the Estate of Chester B. Atkins*

# CONTENTS

Background: Historic RCA Studio B's distinctive checkerboard floor.
*Photo by Bob Delevante*

4

# Introduction

They came as pilgrims, all of them.

They came in hope, and also in fear.

The small room they came to seemed gargantuan. The simple soundboard looked like something from the burgeoning space age. The task at hand was both Herculean and amorphous.

They were called to make magic, without knowing the trick.

Roy Orbison entered, shy and with a soft voice that seemed incapable of rising above the virtuoso sounds of the musicians who gathered to aid him.

The Everly Brothers entered, called upon to send, somehow, blood harmonies into the international stratosphere of rock & roll.

Charley Pride entered, a black man in the segregated South, hoping against lottery odds to use his voice to connect with the hearts and souls of those who figured him a lesser breed of human being.

Dolly Parton entered in a hurried bluster, having rammed her car against the side of the building. She came to turn her singular experience into something universal. She came to make a butterfly transformation, from shielded poverty to glamor and transcendence.

Top: Chet Atkins, c. 1962.

Bottom: Monument Records founder and producer Fred Foster with Roy Orbison, c. 1962. *Photo by Elmer Williams*

Top, L-R: Cadence Records owner and producer Archie Bleyer, guitarist Hank Garland (seated), Don Everly, Phil Everly, bassist Lightnin' Chance, c. 1960.
*Photo by Elmer Williams*

Bottom, L-R: Maxine, Bonnie and Jim Ed Brown, c. 1959.
*Courtesy of Sony Music Archives*

The Browns—Jim Ed, Maxine, and Bonnie—entered, with a plan to make a last-gasp recording before returning to laboring lives in hardscrabble Arkansas. They emerged with "The Three Bells," arguably the smoothest and most elegant recording in country music history.

Elvis Presley entered, a bonus baby of uncommon beauty, uncertain swagger, and a new kind of artistry that would come to redefine popular culture.

Chet Atkins entered, with a key of his very own. He made this place … this little room of tile and baffles and microphones and cables and wood and wire … into a palace of creativity and ascent. In this studio, he conducted the soundtracks to millions of lives and loves, and he established himself—a quiet but whimsical poor boy from East Tennessee—as a marvel of American sound and as a successful, suit-wearing record executive. This building … this pilgrims' mecca we now call Historic RCA Studio B … could also be called "Chet's Place," for it was here that his visions were realized, his guidance heeded, and his mastery confirmed.

This book is about who and when and what, and all of this is important. But there is no need to study these pages for the where or the why.

The where is a humble corner on what is now known as Nashville's Music Row.

And the why?

Why, they came as pilgrims, to touch some gleaming great beyond. They did just that, and they left their fingerprints, along with melodies and harmonies, heartbreak and healing. They came as pilgrims, and now we can, too.

—Peter Cooper

# Home of 1,000 Hits
## Historic RCA Studio B

### By John Rumble

On December 3, 1957, country singer Don Gibson stood before a microphone in a newly built Nashville studio at the corner of 17th Avenue South and Hawkins Street, leased to RCA Records by local businessman Dan Maddox. Poised to record his original song "Oh Lonesome Me," Gibson was backed by drummer Troy Hatcher, vocal quartet the Jordanaires, bassist Joe Zinkan, rhythm guitarist Velma Smith, and guitar ace Chet Atkins, who played electric lead and produced the session. "I just wanted to make 'Oh Lonesome Me' kind of like Don's demo," Atkins later explained. Toward that end, he said, "we miked the bass drum. Up until that time, people just picked up the drums with one mike."

Right: Sleeve for Don Gibson's recording of "Oh Lonesome Me."

Opposite: A small samping of albums recorded at Studio B.
*Photo by Bob Delevante*

On cue, Smith kicked off the performance by playing "a special beat,"
as Atkins had advised, with Zinkan's syncopated bass lines quickly building
the excitement. Atkins spiced the recording with strategic *chunks*, then sailed
into a spirited, rock-tinged break. The Jordanaires sang background chords
("ahh") and punctuated the arrangement with clipped fills ("bah-dee-yah-
bop-bop"). "It was so fresh and so exciting," Atkins reflected in 1989.
"We really hit the bull's eye that time." It was just the kind of recording
to please country fans while reaching beyond the genre's core audience.

An RCA recording artist himself, Atkins had helped Steve Sholes,
RCA's head of country and blues recording, handle sessions in New York
as early as 1947, but as the new Nashville studio's manager of operations,
Atkins was fully accountable for the success or failure of the recording dates
he supervised. Following moves to radio stations in Nashville, Cincinnati,
Denver, and other cities, he landed back in Nashville in 1950. He started
organizing sessions that Sholes produced on regular trips to the Tennessee
capital, and from 1952 RCA paid Atkins a small salary for his efforts.
Sometimes he stepped in to produce sessions himself when Sholes couldn't
make it to Nashville. By the time RCA opened its studio—the place that
would become known eventually as Studio B—in late October 1957, Sholes
had put Atkins in charge, a promotion that increased the pressure on Atkins
to record hits.

Above: The Jordanaires, c. 1955.
Clockwise from upper right: Gordon Stoker, Hugh Jarrett, Neal Matthews Jr., Hoyt Hawkins.

Right: Don Gibson, c. 1957.

## C&W Best Sellers in Stores

FOR SURVEY WEEK ENDING APRIL 12

RECORDS are ranked in order of their current national selling importance at the retail level, as determined by The Billboard's weekly survey of dealers thruout the nation with a high volume of sales in country and western records. When significant action is reported on both sides of record, points are combined to determine position on the chart. In such a case, both sides are listed in bold type, the leading side on top.

| | This Week | Last Week | Weeks on Chart |
|---|---|---|---|
| 1. OH, LONESOME ME (BMI)—Don Gibson | | 1 | 9 |
| I CAN'T STOP LOVING YOU (BMI)—Vic 7133 | | | |
| 2. BALLAD OF A TEENAGE QUEEN (BMI)— | | 2 | 13 |
| Johnny Cash | | | |
| Big River (BMI)—Sun 283 | | | |
| 3. STAIRWAY OF LOVE (ASCAP)—Marty Robbins | | 6 | 3 |
| JUST MARRIED (BMI)—Col 41143 | | 4 | 6 |
| 4. BREATHLESS (BMI)—Jerry Lee Lewis | | 3 | 12 |
| Down the Line (BMI)—Sun 288 | | | |
| 5. DON'T (BMI)—Elvis Presley | | 3 | 12 |
| I BEG OF YOU (BMI)—Vic 7150 | | | |
| 6. CURTAIN IN THE WINDOW (BMI)—Ray Price | | 11 | 3 |
| IT'S ALL YOUR FAULT (BMI)—Col 41105 | | | |
| 7. OH-OH I'M FALLING IN LOVE AGAIN (ASCAP)— | | 5 | 8 |
| Jimmie Rodgers | | | |
| The Long, Hot Summer (ASCAP)—Roulette 4045 | | | |
| 8. WEAR MY RING AROUND YOUR NECK (BMI)— | | — | 1 |
| Elvis Presley | | | |
| Doncha' Think It's Time (BMI)—Vic 7240 | | | |
| 9. YOUR NAME IS BEAUTIFUL (ASCAP)— | | 12 | 6 |
| Carl Smith | | | |
| You're So Easy to Love (BMI)—Col 41092 | | | |
| 10. THE STORY OF MY LIFE (ASCAP)—Marty Robbins | | 7 | 22 |
| Once-a-Week Date (BMI)—Col 41013 | | | |
| 11. STOP THE WORLD (BMI)—Johnnie and Jack | | 9 | 7 |
| Camel Walk Stroll (BMI)—Vic 7137 | | | |
| 12. I CAN'T STOP LOVING YOU (BMI)—Kitty Wells | | 13 | 6 |
| SHE'S NO ANGEL (BMI)—Dec 30551 | | | |
| 13. SEND ME THE PILLOW YOU DREAM ON | | 18 | 2 |
| (BMI)—Hank Locklin | | | |
| Why Don't Haul Off and Love Me (BMI)—Vic 7127 | | | |
| 14. GEISHA GIRL (BMI)—Hank Locklin | | 10 | 35 |
| Livin' Alone (BMI)—Vic 6984 | | | |
| 15. THIS LITTLE GIRL OF MINE (BMI)— | | 8 | 11 |
| Everly Brothers | | | |
| Should We Tell Him (BMI)—Cadence 1342 | | | |
| 16. JUST A LITTLE LONESOME (BMI)— | | 20 | 7 |
| Bobby Helms | | | |
| Love My Lady (BMI)—Dec 30557 | | | |
| 17. WHOLE LOTTA WOMAN (BMI)—Marvin Rainwater | | 15 | 2 |
| Baby, Don't Go (BMI)—M-G-M 12609 | | | |
| 18. IS IT WRONG? (BMI)—Warner Mack | | 14 | 36 |
| Baby Squeeze Me (BMI)—Dec 30301 | | | |
| 19. ANNA MARIE (BMI)—Jim Reeves | | 16 | 12 |
| Everywhere You Go (BMI)—Vic 7070 | | | |
| 20. PINK PEDAL PUSHERS (BMI)—Carl Perkins | | 17 | 3 |
| Jive After Five (BMI)—Col 41131 | | | |

## Most Played C&W by Jockeys

FOR SURVEY WEEK ENDING APRIL 12

SIDES are ranked in order of the greatest number of plays on disk jockey radio shows thruout the country according to The Billboard's weekly survey of top disk jockey shows in all key markets.

| | This Week | Last Week | Weeks on Chart |
|---|---|---|---|
| 1. OH, LONESOME ME—Don Gibson | | 1 | 10 |
| Vic 7133—BMI | | | |
| 2. BALLAD OF A TEENAGE QUEEN—Johnny Cash | | 2 | 14 |
| Sun 283—BMI | | | |
| 3. DON'T—Elvis Presley | | — | 8 |
| Vic 7150—BMI | | | |
| | | 4 | 8 |

As "Oh Lonesome Me" proved, Atkins's country-pop approach worked well. In February 1958 the record began its march to the top of *Billboard* magazine's country charts, where it remained for a whopping eight weeks during its thirty-four-week chart run. The hit scaled the pop charts, too, rising to #7. Recorded at the same session, and issued on the flip side of "Oh Lonesome Me," Gibson's "I Can't Stop Loving You," another original, became a #7 country hit. His double-sided smash confirmed Gibson's status as a star while boosting Atkins's confidence and bringing the new studio instant national visibility.

The studio's opening marked a milestone in Nashville's development as a music center. Based in New York, RCA already maintained studios there and in Chicago, Hollywood, and Camden, New Jersey, but the new facility markedly strengthened the label's commitment to Nashville's emerging music industry. The city's Bradley family had established a studio in 1955 at 804 16th Avenue South, so that the new RCA recording room became the second major enterprise in the neighborhood later called Music Row. Over the following twenty years, RCA Studio B hosted around 18,000 recording sessions. Both RCA's studio and the Bradleys' operation became workshops for hits that embodied the country-pop Nashville Sound. The new style increased country record sales and fueled the dramatic expansion of full-time country radio stations from eighty-one in 1961 to more than six hundred in 1972. Both studios earned worldwide fame for producing musically diverse hits that became firmly grounded in American popular culture. In doing so, the studios helped to secure Nashville's international reputation as Music City, U.S.A.

Charts from the April 21, 1958, issue of *Billboard* magazine.

# America's New *Music Industry*

RCA's new Nashville headquarters reflected the tremendous growth of the American music business during World War II and the decades that followed. This musical explosion outstripped the expansion of the nation's economy as a whole and witnessed the rise of new music centers in cities such as Nashville, Atlanta, Cincinnati, Memphis, Houston, and Detroit. Studio B's debut also mirrored far-reaching changes in American commercial music. Perhaps most important was the increasing dominance of sound recordings, which rapidly replaced live performers on radio and far outdistanced sales of sheet music and songbooks, once the industry's primary consumer products. Record sales rose from $6 million in 1933 to $214 million in 1947; in 1958 this figure jumped to $511 million. By 1959 Americans were spending about $250 million a year on record players, which could be found in almost half of U.S. households.

Millions of fans had money in their pockets, and the thriving radio industry heightened demand for recordings. Advertisers were shifting their spending to the newer medium of television, and in response, radio sharply cut its ranks of expensive live performers and spun records instead.

After the Federal Communications Commission removed its wartime restrictions on new radio licenses, the number of stations climbed from roughly 700 at war's end to some 3,300 in 1957. Many of these were fledgling operations that could not afford live talent. Recordings provided an economical alternative.

By the late 1940s, wartime limits on record production had been lifted, freeing record companies to meet pent-up consumer demand. Major labels RCA, Columbia, and Decca were joined by Capitol in 1942, and MGM (affiliated with the major movie studio) in 1946. Smaller independent labels cropped up across the nation.

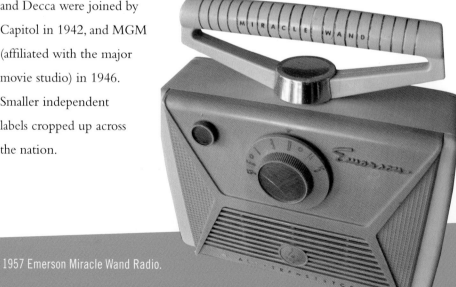

1957 Emerson Miracle Wand Radio.

Teenage star Brenda Lee enjoys her portable record player at home, c. 1957.
*Photo by Elmer Williams*

Tom Parker, far left, with Eddy Arnold, left of placard, and Wally Fowler, in dark shirt and hat, promoting Arnold's show in Florida in 1946.

# Nashville's Postwar *Recording Scene*

From the mid-1940s, major labels and independents tapped Nashville's growing pool of talented performers, many of whom broadcast on WSM, WLAC, and newer radio outlets. Eddy Arnold, lead singer in Grand Ole Opry star Pee Wee King's Golden West Cowboys, left King in 1943 to front his own band, and almost immediately began headlining a network Opry segment sponsored by animal feed supplier Purina. In December 1944, using a WSM studio, the Tennessee Plowboy—as Arnold was known—recorded Nashville's first major-label session since the 1920s. Frank Walker, then president of RCA Victor Records, let Arnold act as his own producer, and the executive's instincts were on target. In 1945, Arnold's rendition of "Each Minute Seems a Million Years" made *Billboard*'s country chart, then based on jukebox play. Between 1945 and 1955 the handsome, smooth-singing star recorded fifty-five Top Ten country hits, twenty

A record press at Nashville's Bullet Plastics, 1947.
*Courtesy of the* Tennessean

of them rising to #1. Arnold cut a good many of these best-sellers in Chicago or New York, but some were recorded in Nashville.

More important for Nashville's reputation were hits recorded at Castle Recording Laboratory, a company formed by three WSM radio engineers around 1946. Using a WSM studio, Aaron Shelton, Carl Jenkins, and George Reynolds recorded "Near You," a high-profile 1947 pop smash that sold two million copies for local orchestra leader Francis Craig on Bullet Records, one of several newly formed Nashville independents.

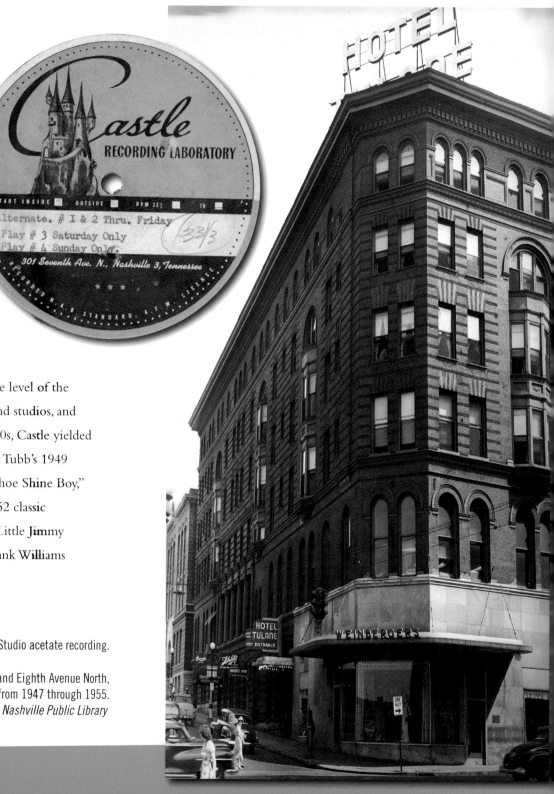

The Castle partners built their own studio on the mezzanine level of the Tulane Hotel, located on Church Street near WSM's offices and studios, and opened for business in the summer of 1947. Into the mid-1950s, Castle yielded such hits as Roy Acuff's "Wabash Cannon Ball" (1947), Ernest Tubb's 1949 chart-topper "Slipping Around," Red Foley's "Chattanoogie Shoe Shine Boy," which went #1 country and #1 pop in 1950, Kitty Wells's 1952 classic "It Wasn't God Who Made Honky Tonk Angels," and hits by Little Jimmy Dickens, George Morgan, Carl Smith, and Marty Robbins. Hank Williams cut most of his commercial releases at Castle.

Above: Label from an early Castle Studio acetate recording.

Right: The Hotel Tulane at the corner of Church Street and Eighth Avenue North, home of the Castle studio from 1947 through 1955.
*Courtesy of the Nashville Room at the Nashville Public Library*

Castle's success prompted Owen Bradley to establish a studio with his brother Harold, a versatile guitarist who began playing sessions in 1946. After making industrial films in a building at Second Avenue South and Lindsley, the Bradleys opened a recording studio in Nashville's Hillsboro Village neighborhood around 1953. With Decca producer Paul Cohen guaranteeing to schedule a minimum of a hundred sessions annually, they remodeled an old house on 16th Avenue South during 1954 and 1955, and created a studio within its walls. In short order, they created a second studio in a surplus military Quonset hut set up behind the house. Soon, a stream of hits emerged from these two rooms, officially called the Bradley Film and Recording Studios. Most Columbia artists did the bulk of their recording there, and after Owen Bradley became Decca's country recording chief in 1958, so did many Decca acts. Like RCA, the Bradleys rented their studios to other labels, whose artists recorded hits in many musical genres.

Top: Slim Whitman recording at the Bradley Studio, c. 1956.
Left to right: Bob Moore (bass), Thumbs Carllile (guitar),
Owen Bradley (piano, in background), Harold Bradley (seated, guitar),
Whitman, Lillian Van Hunt (fiddle), unidentified (steel guitar).
*Photo by Elmer Williams*

Bottom: View of the Bradley Studios' Quonset Hut, c. 1956.

# RCA Strengthens Its
## *Nashville Presence*

Although RCA's Nashville team was running for touchdowns by 1958, the label had been relatively slow to join the city's fertile postwar recording scene. As part of the Radio Corporation of America, a major conglomerate involved in radio, television, and recording, RCA Victor Records was contractually bound to use union engineers certified by the National Association of Broadcast Employees and Technicians (NABET). Moreover, these engineers wanted to use equipment they had designed and built. To record in Nashville, RCA had to find local entrepreneurs willing to accommodate RCA producers and NABET engineers who came down

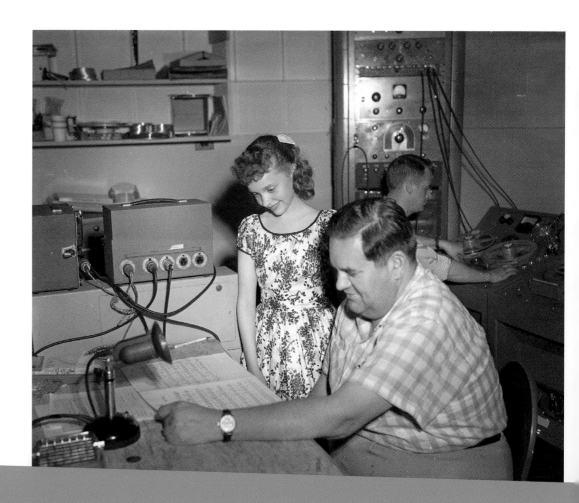

Recording artist Libby Horne with RCA executive Steve Sholes and unidentified engineer, Methodist Television, Radio, and Film Commission (TRAFCO) studio, c. 1957.
*Photo by Elmer Williams*

Chet Atkins with the Browns, TRAFCO Building, c. 1956.
Left to right: Buddy Harman (drums); Velma Smith (guitar);
Roy "Junior" Huskey (bass); Atkins; Maxine, Bonnie, and Jim Ed Brown.
*Photo by Elmer Williams*

from New York periodically. Radio syndicators Charles and Bill Brown were amenable, and RCA held sessions at the Browns' studio on Fourth Avenue North as early as 1950. After the Browns closed their doors, RCA shifted to Thomas Productions on Thirteenth Avenue North. In January 1955, the label set up shop on McGavock Street with a studio and office space rented from the Television, Radio, and Film Commission (TRAFCO) of the Methodist Church.

Assisted by Atkins, RCA country recording director Steve Sholes used all of these facilities. From January 1955 through October 1957 his artists, including Eddy Arnold, the Browns, Don Gibson, Johnnie & Jack, Hank Locklin, Jim Reeves, Homer and Jethro, and Hank Snow recorded numerous country hits at the TRAFCO Building. In 1957 Atkins recorded "Mister Sandman," his first chart-making disc. The Statesmen and the Blackwood Brothers, among other gospel acts, used the TRAFCO studio as well.

Left to right: Chet Atkins, bassist Bob Moore, and recording artist June Webb, TRAFCO Building, 1957.
*Photo by Elmer Williams*

# The Hits

A sampling of hits recorded by RCA artists in Nashville's TRAFCO Building studio from November 1954 through October 1957.

**Eddy Arnold**

    "That Do Make It Nice"         #1     1955

**Chet Atkins**

    "Mr. Sandman"         #13     1955

**The Browns**

    "I Heard the Bluebirds Sing"         #4     1957

**Don Gibson**

    "Blue Blue Day"         #1     1958

**Hank Locklin**

    "Send Me the Pillow You Dream On"         #5     1958

**Elvis Presley**

    "Heartbreak Hotel"         #1     1956

**Jim Reeves**

    "Four Walls"         #1     1957

**Hank Snow**

    "Hula Rock"         #5     1956

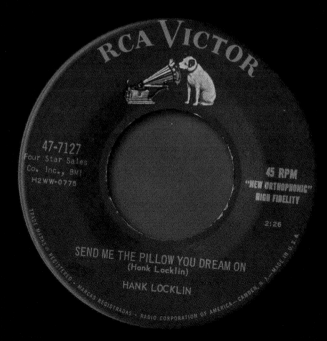

# Elvis Presley and Country's
## *Rock & Roll Challenge*

During the mid-1950s, however, the RCA artist who had the greatest industry-wide impact was Elvis Presley. As a Sun Records star, the hip, handsome singer known as the "Hillbilly Cat" fused country music with rhythm & blues while leading Sun's pack of rockabillies, including Johnny Cash, Jerry Lee Lewis, and Carl Perkins.

Presley got strong support among country disc jockeys and starred briefly on Shreveport's KWKH *Louisiana Hayride*, but as the nation's leading rock & roll hitmaker, he helped depress country record sales. Combined with the spread of TV ownership—which kept many Americans at home during the evenings—the popularity of rock & roll movement lowered concert gate receipts for many country acts, especially older performers with styles that began to seem dated to younger listeners' ears.

Right: Elvis on the cover of *TV Guide*, September 9, 1956.

Opposite page: Sam Phillips and Elvis Presley at Memphis Recording Service, 1956.
*Photo by George Pierce. Courtesy of the Sam Phillips Family*

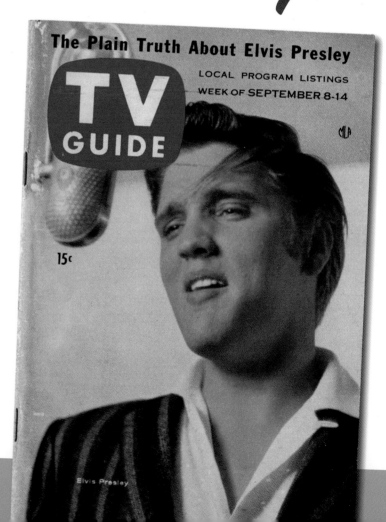

The Plain Truth About Elvis Presley

LOCAL PROGRAM LISTINGS
WEEK OF SEPTEMBER 8-14

TV GUIDE

15¢

Elvis Presley

FOUR WALLS · I KNOW (and You Know)
THE GODS WERE ANGRY WITH ME · LOOK BEHIND YOU

EPA-4062

FOUR WALLS
JIM REEVES

RCA VICTOR
A "NEW ORTHOPHONIC" HIGH FIDELITY RECORDING

VOL. II
EL RANCHO GRANDE
LA PALOMA
GRANDFATHER'S CLOCK
THE LOVER'S FAREWELL

EPA 1-1435

HANK SNOW'S
COUNTRY
GUITAR

RCA VICTOR
A "NEW ORTHOPHONIC" HIGH FIDELITY RECORDING

To meet the challenge, RCA executives and their counterparts at other labels pursued three basic strategies. Seeking to retain country's longstanding, musically conservative audience, producers re-tooled the sounds of hard-country artists by recording them in better studios with innovative session musicians and engineers.

A second approach was a fresh twist on the well-established practice of courting a larger adult audience with pop-influenced country singers. By 1956 country producers were downplaying fiddles and steel guitars and adding piano, backing voices, and string arrangements to shape more broadly accessible sounds. On February 27, 1957, for example, RCA's velvet-voiced Jim Reeves cut "Four Walls," one of the earliest expressions of the Nashville Sound's country-pop blend. Backed by the Jordanaires vocal quartet, Reeves recorded this classic at the TRAFCO studio, with Atkins producing. "It was his idea to get in close to the microphone and get that intimate sound," Atkins said. "It wasn't mine. I latched onto it once I heard how good it sounded." The single became a #1 country hit, rose to #11 on the pop charts, and led to Reeves's pop radio show, fed to the ABC network from WSM in 1957 and 1958. The record also set the pattern for the singer's later hits, almost all of them recorded at Studio B.

Covers for extended-play (EP) 45-rpm recordings
by Jim Reeves and Hank Snow, 1957.

A third strategy was to sign rockabilly acts—and thereby gain market share among teenagers who were snapping up records right and left. In November 1955, RCA's Sholes had paid $35,000—then an astounding sum—for Presley's Sun contract. Some industry observers considered the move foolish and predicted Sholes's imminent downfall, but Presley proved them wrong by selling millions of records right out of the gate. His first RCA session, held at the TRAFCO building on January 10, 1956, yielded "Heartbreak Hotel," which shot to #1 country and #1 pop. Six more chart-topping Presley discs followed during 1956 and 1957. The singer would go on to record more than two hundred sides in Studio B, including hits essential to his iconic status in world popular culture.

Cover for 1956 RCA extended-play disc including Elvis Presley's smash hit "Heartbreak Hotel."

Left to right: Promoter Bob Neal, Sun Records founder Sam Phillips, RCA attorney H. Coleman Tily III, Elvis Presley, and Presley's manager, Colonel Tom Parker, on the day Phillips sold Presley's contract to RCA, November 21, 1955. *Courtesy of the Sam Phillips Family*

# From McGavock Street
## to Music Row

Despite their success at the TRAFCO building, Sholes and Atkins disliked the studio. "It had a curved ceiling," Atkins explained in 1992. "When you'd play a bass note, it would amplify it, and it would come back at you and get in all the other mikes." Scheduling sessions around Methodist Church projects was sometimes problematic, and some church leaders weren't happy about recording the devil's music while educators were working on church publications. "Whenever Piano Red [Willie Lee Perryman], a blues singer, was pounding the keyboard and bellowing 'You Got the Right String Baby but the Wrong Yo-Yo,'" RCA sales executive Brad McCuen said, "I felt sorry for the poor guys upstairs trying to write Sunday School lessons. It just wasn't a good situation." Sholes and Atkins agreed that it was time for a new studio where RCA could control the schedule and upgrade the equipment. The string of hits they had achieved—especially the profits Presley generated—helped them persuade label bosses to accommodate them.

Enter Dan Maddox, a sharp-eyed Nashville businessman with diverse interests in finance, real estate, and construction. As Maddox recalled, "I was looking for some investments, and the bank asked me to look at some property [on McGavock Street] and make them an offer on it . . .

So I did. It had two tenants in it. One was the Radio and Film Commission of the Methodist Church, and the other was RCA Victor . . . Both of them were unhappy because they had outgrown their space. So, being a Methodist myself, I favored the church." Maddox offered to put up a new building to house an RCA studio, and the label agreed. With the promise of a long-term tenant, Maddox began work on a building at the corner of 17th Avenue South and Hawkins Street in the summer of 1957. William "Bill" Miltenberg, a leading engineer at RCA's New York headquarters, sketched preliminary plans on a restaurant napkin. The structure measured 65 feet by 150 feet. According to Maddox, the cost came to $39,515.

In late October, RCA New York engineer Les Chase worked with Nashville engineer Selby Coffeen in setting up tape machines, a mixing board, and other equipment. Evidently, Columbia Records' Jo Ann Davis was the first artist to use the new space, on October 29. The next day, RCA's Hank Snow cut "I'm Hurtin' All Over" and "My Memory," both unreleased for many years. "The Party of the Second Part," also cut on October 30, was later paired with Snow's 1959 rendition of "The Last Ride" on a single release.

## Recording Studio in Expanded Quarters

—Staff photo by Joe Rudis

Radio Corp. of America's recording studio is being moved into this new expanded quarters at 800 Seventeenth ave., S., from 1525 McGavock st. It is equipped with the latest innovations in sound equipment. It will hold open house during the annual disc jockey convention later this year.

In its issue for November 4, 1957, Nashville-based trade magazine *Music Reporter* noted that RCA's new Nashville studio was "already booking a heavy schedule of recording dates." Expanding the beachhead established by the Bradley studios two years earlier, the new RCA facility helped to attract other music enterprises to the neighborhood eventually known as Music Row.

Studio B's completion in 1957 was especially timely, not only for the new enterprise itself, but also for the Bradleys and other Nashville recording entrepreneurs who followed. In 1956 Castle's days were numbered by a WSM decree that staff abandon their outside businesses or give up their positions with WSM. The Tulane Hotel, home to Castle, was about to be razed, and with long WSM service records and pensions to protect, the Castle partners elected to terminate their company around the time Studio B was ready to host some of Nashville's growing number of recording sessions.

The *Tennessean*, October 26, 1957.

# Nashville Sound Classics, 1958-1959
## Bill Porter Joins RCA's Team

The hot streak Don Gibson began in 1957 with "Oh Lonesome Me" and "I Can't Stop Loving You" burned on in the years following, when Gibson notched five more Top Ten records. Background singers, Gibson's solid lead vocals, and tight instrumental support heightened the impact of his original material.

The year 1959 proved to be especially successful for RCA Nashville, though it certainly didn't begin that way. Underneath his calm exterior Chet Atkins was a sensitive artist, and he sometimes lost his temper under the pressures of finding songs, producing a large talent roster, and making his own records.

Left: Chet Atkins and Bill Porter at Studio B's mixing board, c. 1962.

Opposite: Left to right: Bill Porter, Acuff-Rose Publications president Wesley Rose, unidentified, songwriter Boudleaux Bryant, Studio B, c. 1962.
*Photo by Elmer Williams*

Early in '59 he lashed out at engineer Bob Ferris, who often irritated his colleagues. Atkins took a swing at Ferris and missed, hitting a piece of equipment instead. No one remembers exactly what set Atkins off, but the incident led the engineers' union to close the studio while Ferris trained a replacement.

Work soon resumed, though, with former Nashville TV cameraman Bill Porter as chief engineer. Porter quickly became one of RCA Nashville's greatest assets. Just as Atkins taught Porter to monitor recordings at a lower volume level—which let both men hear a full range of frequencies more accurately—the producer readily absorbed Porter's knowledge of microphone types and placement, mixing consoles and techniques, and echo effects.

From the outset, Porter faced serious challenges in capturing some of the label's best vocalists on tape. "The Browns were a real soft sound," he explained, "and they had a beautiful harmony. But if they tried to project that harmony, the balance would just disappear. As a result of that, it was quite difficult to keep the band's music out of [the vocal] microphone, because you had to open the mike up so much, everything poured in. It was really a struggle to keep everything as quiet as I possibly could. Chet, many times, would want [the band] to play a little bit louder and harder, and I can understand why, but it would start to kill the sound, definitely. When that happens, the

The challenges of acoustics in the early days of Studio B. Columbia recording artist Jo Ann Davis, unidentified guitarist, drummer Buddy Harman, and bassist Bob Moore, October 29, 1957.
*Photo by Elmer Williams*

intimate sound you get on the instruments disappears because you've got the distance from the instrument to the vocal mike, and the sound travels across the room, so the time distance . . . makes it sound like the band's in the next room. It's one of those things you were locked in with . . . There was no way of isolating things like you can today. Right up until I left at the end of 1963, RCA wouldn't put the money into vocal booths. I had a couple of acoustical flats, which were basically nothing but that old-fashioned ceiling tile with holes in it, plastered right to the wood. That's all we had. There wasn't very much you could do with that!

"[Assistant engineer] Tommy Strong and I did a little bit of research to try to figure some way—anything we could do to help the room. Since the drums were pretty well set up all the way, we experimented. We put microphones up in different places around the room while one of us beat on the drums, and we looked at the VU [volume unit] meters and found the places where the sound was minimal. We'd mark X's on the floor, for acoustic guitar, and the vocal [and] back-up vocal, so we'd get as much isolation as possible."

Early Studio B equipment.
Top: This Teletronix compressor-limiter kept high-volume notes from saturating the recording tape.

Bottom: Ampex 300 tape recorder.
*Photos by Bob Delevante*

Eventually, Porter and Strong made additional improvements. "I got Mr. Hines [Ed Hines, who booked sessions for non-RCA labels] to let me get about $60 out of petty cash," Porter continued. "I went out and bought a bunch of acoustical panels, and I took those acoustical panels and made 'em triangular—cut 'em up—and hung 'em at different heights across the room. (I knew enough about acoustics to be dangerous. That's really it.) But the sound difference was phenomenal! **They kinda dubbed those things 'Porter's Pyramids.' They didn't look very good, but they worked.** Breaking up the standing waves in the room—that's all it was doing. A standing wave is where a sound will reflect off the room and come back to the original point, and you'll get cancellation points across that distance and additions across that distance, so some notes will be louder and some will be softer by virtue of the room. The pyramids helped some of that. A cheap way of doing it. I hate to say it, but RCA of New York, their standard answer was, 'You're doing a good job with what you got. Leave it alone.' That's all I ever got from 'em . . . No vocal booth, no drum booth, no nothing! Everything was out in the open. Acoustical panel baffles about four feet high around the drums—that was all!"

Top right: Eddy Arnold with Dottie Dillard, of the Anita Kerr Singers, 1960s.
Bottom right: Artist unidentified. Ray Edenton at left, 1960s.

Porter was a master at balancing instruments and background voices and putting them in proper relationship to the lead vocal. His goal was to create an ambient sound that replicated what a listener would hear sitting about eight rows from the stage at a concert. While making music publishers' demos, he and Strong experimented with microphones to learn which ones sounded best with particular instruments. Except for second- or third-generation masters, it was impossible to overdub after a session was over, nor was it possible to re-mix after the fact. Early on, engineers had to mix as recordings were made.

Porter's abilities were critical in recording "The Three Bells," in a June 1959 session with Jim Ed Brown and his sisters Maxine and Bonnie. The Browns had signed with RCA in 1956, but in spite of encouraging results, they tired of grinding tours and low-paying show dates. They were planning to quit the business and attend to family responsibilities after one final session. French chanteuse Edith Piaf recorded the song as "Les Trois Cloche," yet her version was far too long for a three-minute single, so Anita Kerr, Atkins's principal arranger, made judicious edits. Complementing the Browns' smooth three-part harmony, she led her Anita Kerr Singers on background vocals evoking the church bells essential to the storyline. All in all, it was a classic Nashville Sound recording. Atkins thought the performance had great sales potential, and told the Browns not to leave professional music just yet.

Like Sholes, Atkins often had trouble getting help from RCA's New York-based promotion department. "This time," Jim Ed Brown said, "he went up to New York and told the corporate officials that if they didn't get on this song and promote it, he was going to leave the company." Partly as a result, it topped both country and pop charts and put the Browns onto network television and international tours. "Scarlet Ribbons (for Her Hair)" and "The Old Lamplighter," also crossover hits, followed in 1959 and 1960, respectively.

Recorded October 15, 1959, Jim Reeves's million-selling "He'll Have to Go" was yet another crossover smash crafted at Studio B with Atkins producing and Porter at the console. Distilling the essence of the Nashville Sound, the recording framed the star's rich baritone with a minimalist background featuring piano and vibes; Kerr's vocal quartet artfully took the place of strings. The hit spent thirty-four weeks on *Billboard*'s country chart during 1959 and 1960, fourteen of them at #1; during its twenty-three weeks on the pop chart, the recording climbed to #2.

This 1960 album captures the broad audience appeal of crossover act the Browns.

# "Magical, is what it was."

## By Fred Foster

### Member, Country Music Hall of Fame

Studio B was a great studio to work in. First, it wasn't overly large, so there was an intimacy about it. Now, on some of the bigger productions, like with Roy Orbison, to support the artist I had a full rhythm section plus vibes, eight background singers, and fourteen strings, so that's more than thirty people. On those sessions, we virtually filled the studio, and you got real friendly with your neighbors, being almost on top of each other. But it worked. And the magic came from the people who were making the records, and enjoyed playing there. And it came from our engineer, Bill Porter, who understood electronics and acoustics and how to get the right balance and blend of sounds, and the right amount of echo. He was willing to try anything we wanted to try.

I like to say that the best part of the building was the broken water fountain, which had copper pipes near it, waiting to be used in fixing it. When Boots Randolph was recording "Yakety Sax," Bill Pursell was playing piano. I took one copper tube and laid it across the strings. Bill played a few bars, and it sounded pretty good; the pipe added to the rhythm. Then I tried adding two pipes, and then three, but I took the third one off since the effect was too great. With two pipes, the higher-pitched strings sounded good, but the lower-pitched strings were still rattling. So we went in the bathroom and got a bunch of paper towels, and then stuffed them under the low strings. We wound up with a Top 40 pop hit in 1963, and it later became the theme music for the *Benny Hill Show*.

I founded Monument Records in 1958, and soon moved from Washington, DC, to Nashville. Our first hit came in 1959 with Billy Grammer's "Gotta Travel On," which made the Top Five on both the country and pop charts. That alone makes Studio B a special place for me. But I was lucky enough to produce quite a few hits there, including Roy Orbison's early 1960s hits, some of which became international best-sellers. So I have a lot of happy memories of RCA Studio B. As I said, I think it's magical.

Monument hitmakers Billy Grammer (standing, left) and Billy Graves (standing, right) confer with Monument president Fred Foster (in suit), studio musical director Bob Moore (far right), and the Anita Kerr Singers (from left): Louis Nunley, Gil Wright, Kerr, and Dottie Dillard. Studio B, c. 1960.
*Photo by Elmer Williams*

# *High* Gear

RCA Nashville roared into the 1960s with still more hits. "Please Help Me, I'm Falling" (1960) showcased Hank Locklin's yearning tenor vocal style with distinctive piano effects. Co-writer Don Robertson sang on the demo he sent to Atkins, accompanying himself on piano with a "slipnote" technique featuring grace notes similar to steel guitar slides. Initially, session pianist Floyd Cramer thought it was corny, but Atkins persuaded him otherwise, and the Locklin recording went to #1 country and #8 pop, deeply embedding the slipnote style in country music. Atkins then urged Cramer to write his own slipnote song, and Cramer's 1960 crossover hit "Last Date" (#11 country, #2 pop) established his signature sound as both artist and studio musician.

From the mid-1950s, Atkins worked with Skeeter Davis to create her own harmony by adding new vocal parts to second-generation master tapes as the original masters were transferred to them. In 1960, Davis sang a harmony line to her recording of "Am I That Easy to Forget?," and she later told Atkins she had dreamed about

Above right: This 1960 Skeeter Davis album features "Am I That Easy to Forget?," including two harmony parts Davis sang herself.

Right: Davis recording in Studio B, c. 1960.

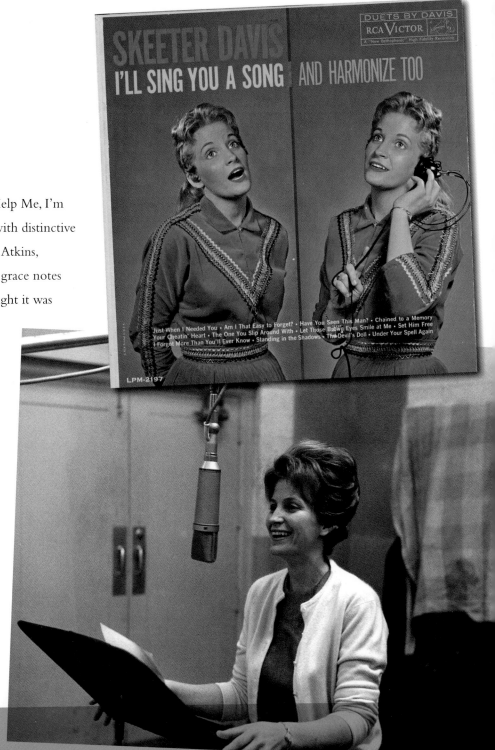

a third part. Davis described his reaction in her autobiography, *Bus Fare to Kentucky*: "'Look,' Chet said, almost angrily. 'You're the artist. Do you understand that? What I'm saying, Skeeter, is trust your own creative judgment.'" Though he had already sent the second-generation master to New York, Atkins was able to call it back; Davis added the third part to a third-generation master that resulted in a #11 country hit.

Steve Sholes had high praise for the man he'd put in charge of Studio B. "In terms of long-range and multiple-artists benefits for the label," *Billboard* reported in its issue for September 12, 1960, "Sholes regards Atkins as his most important coup. As one of the label's hottest artists and as head of the Nashville operation, [he] has been producing better than 50 percent of the label's singles hits." In October, the magazine named Atkins its Country and Western Man of the Year.

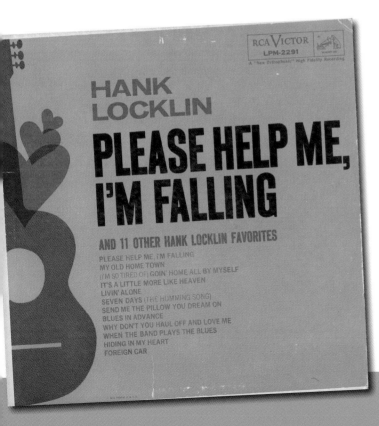

Left: This 1960 Hank Locklin album capitalized on his 1960 chart-topping single "Please Help Me, I'm Falling."

Right: *Billboard*, October 31, 1960.

## OCTOBER 31, 1960

# Chet Atkins Named C. & W. Man of Year

RCA Victor's Chet Atkins has been selected as The Billboard's "Country and Western Man of The Year" for 1960, because, as both artist and a.&r. man, he has long stood for musical quality and has contributed greatly to the ever-widening interest in country music thruout the popular field.

Atkins is deeply rooted in the country scene, first, as a guitarist and, second, as a knowledgeable judge of material in his a.&r. capacity as a maker of hits.

Chet was born in Luttrell, Tenn., some 20 miles from Knoxville, June 20, 1924. His musical education came naturally, for his father was a teacher of piano and voice. As a teen-ager, Chet joined the broadcasting studios of WNOX, Knoxville, and played with two groups at the station, including a Dixieland jazz combo. Afterwards, he moved to WLW, Cincinnati; then to WPTF, Raleigh, N. C., and

**CHET ATKINS**

after a few more stops to WSM, Nashville, where he became a regular, in 1950, on "Grand Ole Opry." It was at this time, too, that he began doing the record producing work that led him, under the aegis of Victor a.&r. exec. Steve Sholes, to the executive position he now holds in the Nashville operation for the company.

**Aided Many Others**

Besides a number of hits of his own, the foremost of which are "Boo Boo Stick Beat" and "Mint Julip," Chet has been involved in any number of chart toppers by other RCA Victor artists. Under his supervision the Browns have produced "Three Bells"; Don Gibson has sung his way to stardom on "Lonesome Me," and Jim Reeves recorded "Four Walls," "Blue Boy" and "He'll Have to Go," to name just a few. All of these artists, plus many more, look to Chet for advice and direction when they enter the recording studio.

Perhaps most important in his role as a guitarist, of which there have been thousands thruout his career, was his appearance as guest soloist with the Atlanta Symphony. Chet was also scheduled to appear at the last ill-fated Newport Jazz Festival, but because of the riots his combo's appearance was postponed. Atkins' desire to play was so great that he performed, session style, on the lawn of his hotel there and the proceedings were caught live, by RCA Victor. This recording is Atkin's current Victor LP release, "After the Riots at Newport."

Besides his a.&r. and guitar activities, Atkins also teaches and designs guitars and is author of a guitar methods handbook.

# Nashville *Cats*

Chet Atkins, was quick to credit Nashville's studio professionals for his good fortune. Eventually known as the "Nashville Cats," their creativity and improvisational skills supported a wide range of vocal styles while working smoothly and efficiently. "The musicians in this town will cut you a hit if you don't get in their way too much," Atkins was fond of saying. Into the early 1970s, the vast majority of sessions used a small group of first-call pros, including Atkins and fellow guitarists Norman Blake, Harold Bradley, Jimmy Capps, Jimmy Colvard, Ray Edenton, and Hank Garland. Other guitar slingers were Jerry Kennedy, Grady Martin, Wayne Moss, Jerry Reed, Billy Sanford, Pete Wade, Paul Yandell, and Chip Young. Floyd "Lightnin'" Chance, Junior Huskey, Bob Moore, Ernie Newton, Joe Osborn, Henry Strzelecki, and Joe Zinkan were first-rate bass players, while top drummers included Kenny Buttrey, Jerry Carrigan, Farris Coursey, and Buddy Harman.

Top right:  Chet Atkins and harmonica ace Charlie McCoy.
*Courtesy of Sony Music Archives*

Bottom right: Some of Nashville's "A-Team" at RCA Studio B, 1960s.
Left to right (standing): Ray Edenton, Jerry Smith, Charlie McCoy, Henry Strzelecki.
Kneeling: Chet Atkins (left), Buddy Harman (right).
*Courtesy of Merle Atkins Russell and the estate of Chester B. Atkins*

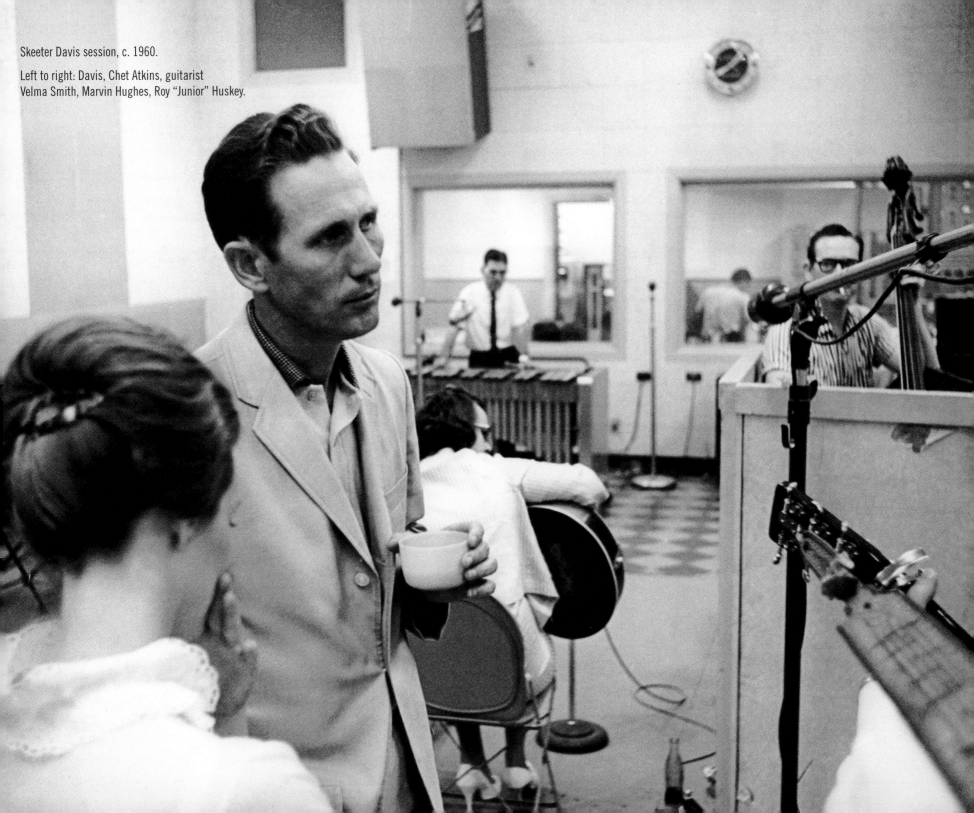

Skeeter Davis session, c. 1960.

Left to right: Davis, Chet Atkins, guitarist
Velma Smith, Marvin Hughes, Roy "Junior" Huskey.

Keyboardists David Briggs, Floyd Cramer, Marvin Hughes, Ron Oates, Bill Pursell, and Hargus "Pig" Robbins were also essential, as were steel guitar players Stu Basore, Pete Drake, Buddy Emmons, Lloyd Green, Don Helms, John Hughey, Shot Jackson, Weldon Myrick, and Hal Rugg. Banjo pickers included Sonny Osborne, Earl Scruggs, Bobby Thompson, and Buck Trent; fiddle duties were typically fulfilled by Vassar Clements, Johnny Gimble, Tommy Jackson, Dale Potter, and Buddy Spicher. String ensembles sometimes consisted of Nashville Symphony members and were often led by Tennessee State University professor Brenton Banks, Lillian Van Hunt, and Sheldon Kurland. Jethro Burns on mandolin, Boots Randolph on saxophone, and multi-instrumentalist Charlie McCoy on harmonica all increased the versatility of Music City's A-Team players.

At one time or another, virtually every top Nashville session player or background vocalist recorded in Studio B, creating lasting memories in the process. "I cut my first Nashville session there backing up Ann-Margret," said McCoy, "and the first big hit I played on, Roy Orbison's 'Candy Man,' was recorded there, too."

Above: Floyd Cramer, c. 1961.

Right: Studio B's Steinway B classic grand, built in 1942 and played by Floyd Cramer, Hargus "Pig" Robbins, and other pianists on numerous hits. Elvis Presley often played this piano while warming up with the Jordanaires.
*Photo by Bob Delevante*

By the mid-1960s, the Nashville Edition vocal group was finding steady session work. Tenor singer Joe Babcock described their approach, also typical of the Jordanaires and the Anita Kerr Singers, whose impromptu arrangements were written by Neal Matthews Jr. and Kerr, respectively: "We usually heard the song on demo once or twice and were required to learn and record four songs in three hours," Babcock said. "I made the charts of songs' harmonic progressions and arranged for our group. We usually learned the song, the chords, and the phrasing, as well as my arrangement, and were able to get it down in a few takes. In the early days there were only four tracks, so our group was on one mike and we had to make sure we were balanced within ourselves. There was no such thing as Pro Tools [software], so we had to be in tune, phrase with the artist, and have the perfect balance of voices in regard to volume and tone for it to be a professional sound. Everyone in the group had a gifted ear, which was a necessity in Nashville for that kind of work, and still is."

Top left: Don Gibson session, c. 1961. Left to right: Gibson, unidentified, Neal Matthews Jr., Johnny Smith, Harold Bradley.

Left: Roy Orbison session, early 1960s. Left to right, standing: Orbison, bassist and musical director Bob Moore, Anita Kerr. String players include Lillian Van Hunt (next to microphone) and Brenton Banks (partly obscured by bow). *Photo by Elmer Williams*

Right: Drum sticks and glove used by Kenny Buttrey.

Bottom:
Two of Charlie McCoy's harmonicas.

*Photos by Bob Delevante*

Along with professional studio players and singers, Atkins gave kudos to RCA staff engineers, especially Bill Porter. "He had great ears, and he was a great technical man," Atkins said. "He's the best engineer I ever had." To be sure, Porter achieved remarkable results with limited technology. The equipment installed soon after he arrived in 1959 had three output channels, but three-track master tapes were then used to create a back-up "safety" tape. Before stereo FM radio came into vogue in the late 1960s, engineers usually mixed three-track tapes down to a single output channel routed to a monaural tape machine. These tapes were used to create 45-rpm singles for AM radio broadcasting and retail sales. For albums, engineers sometimes mixed the three-track tapes to two-track masters, and included the lead vocal on both the left and right tracks. When the recordings were played, the human ear perceived the vocals as coming from a "phantom" center track.

Opposite, left to right: Weldon Myrick, Chet Atkins, Henry Strzelecki, Jerry Carrigan, Charlie McCoy, Sonny Osborne (banjo), Wayne Moss (far right, guitar). Seated in front are Anita Kerr Singers Louis Nunley, Dottie Dillard, and Gil Wright. Bill Pursell and Priscilla Reed behind Dillard.
*Courtesy of Sony Music Archives*

Chet and his assistant,
Juanita Jones, c. 1965.

# Chet Atkins, Producer

In choosing material for sessions, Bill Porter emphasized, Chet Atkins "didn't want to hear a finished demo," which might pre-dispose him to recreate its arrangement. After selecting songs in consultation with the artist, Atkins lined up session personnel. "Chet picked what he felt was the cream of the crop for what he was doing," said second engineer Tommy Strong. "Then the musicians would devise who did what. He'd give all of them the opportunity to contribute. Most of the time, the musicians worked out 'head' arrangements. Except for strings or horns, nothing was really pre-arranged."

So understated was Atkins's manner that casual observers sometimes thought he "didn't do anything." In fact, Atkins knew his own reputation as top-flight musician and producer could be intimidating, and he deliberately created a laid-back studio atmosphere. "He'd be playing his guitar or reading," Ray Edenton recalled,

Golf club at the ready, Jerry Reed welcomes Chet Atkins to a 1960s session.

"but he was aware of everything that went on. You couldn't put anything by him, musically. He'd hear something and come on the talk-back and tell you to slow it down, speed it up, try a different instrument on a certain part. But Chet wasn't bashful. He'd give you a chance to try something else, but if he didn't hear what he wanted, he didn't hesitate to come out into the studio and show you."

Studio guitarist Harold Bradley summarized Atkins's producing style by comparing it with his brother Owen's: "Chet and Owen shared the concept that the artist was the diamond, and we were the setting. Chet could demonstrate his ideas on his guitar or a fiddle, for instance, but he wanted to hear our ideas first, and then he picked out what he wanted out of what we gave him. Owen was much more hands on; he was much more likely to come out into the studio and shape the record. It was a case of two different methods, and both methods worked."

Top left: Hank Locklin, Chet Atkins, and Floyd Cramer, Studio B, c. 1960.

Above: Atkins and Perry Como, early 1970s.

Bottom left: Atkins with Hank Snow, RCA Studio A, c. 1970.

Ray Walker, bass singer for the Jordanaires, had this to say: "Like Owen, Chet depended on the artists to deliver. With an established artist, he and the artist would know each other well enough that he didn't have to say much during a session. Of course, if he couldn't hear the artist on a particular word or phrase, he'd say, 'I can't understand that word. Would you mind doing that part over?' With a newly signed artist, he worked things out beforehand so they understood each other. We enjoyed working with him and for him and with the artists that he had. He was always very kind about saying, 'Why don't you lay out on this line,' or 'Put something in right there . . . Chet gave you time to blossom,' Walker continued. "He respected musicians and singers. He knew what they were up against. We were all under pressure, within a limited time frame, to get what we had in our heads onto the recordings we were making."

Top: Atkins and Charlie Rich, Studio B, c. 1964.
*Courtesy of Sony Music Archives*

Above: Atkins and sitar master Havishar Rao, Studio B, 1967.
*Courtesy of Sony Music Archives*

Right: Atkins and Jerry Reed, early 1970s.
*Courtesy of Merle Atkins Russell and the estate of Chester B. Atkins*

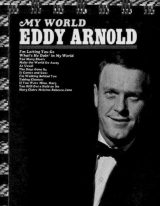

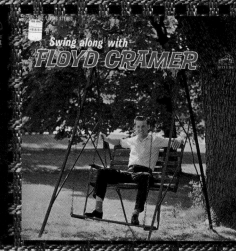

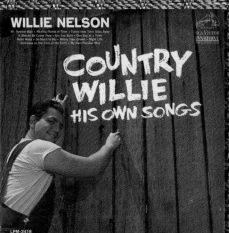

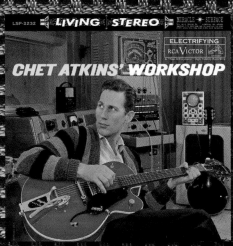

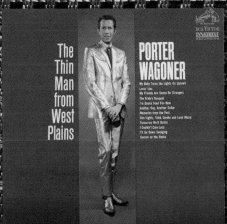

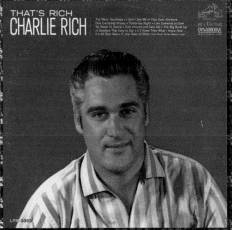

# Is It Gonna Happen?
## *Elvis Returns*

From 1958 to 1960, army service interrupted Elvis Presley's career, but when he started recording again, Studio B's broadening reputation—and Bill Porter's proven abilities—led Steve Sholes to bring RCA's top-selling singer back to Nashville for his first post-army sessions. On March 20, 1960, when Presley and manager Colonel Tom Parker rolled up to Studio B's back door in a chartered bus, Parker's customary security guards were on hand to greet them. In the studio Presley relaxed by telling army stories, joking, and gathering around the piano with the Jordanaires to warm up by singing gospel songs. Two years had passed since any of the executives or studio musicians had heard Presley make a record.

"There was such an awful tension in the control room, you could just feel it," Porter remembered. "I was into trying to get a balance on the mix and everything, and then I kept feeling this pressure. I tried to look behind me,

Right: This 1960 album announced Presley's return from the army.

Opposite: Notation for Elvis Presley's hit "Are You Lonesome Tonight?"

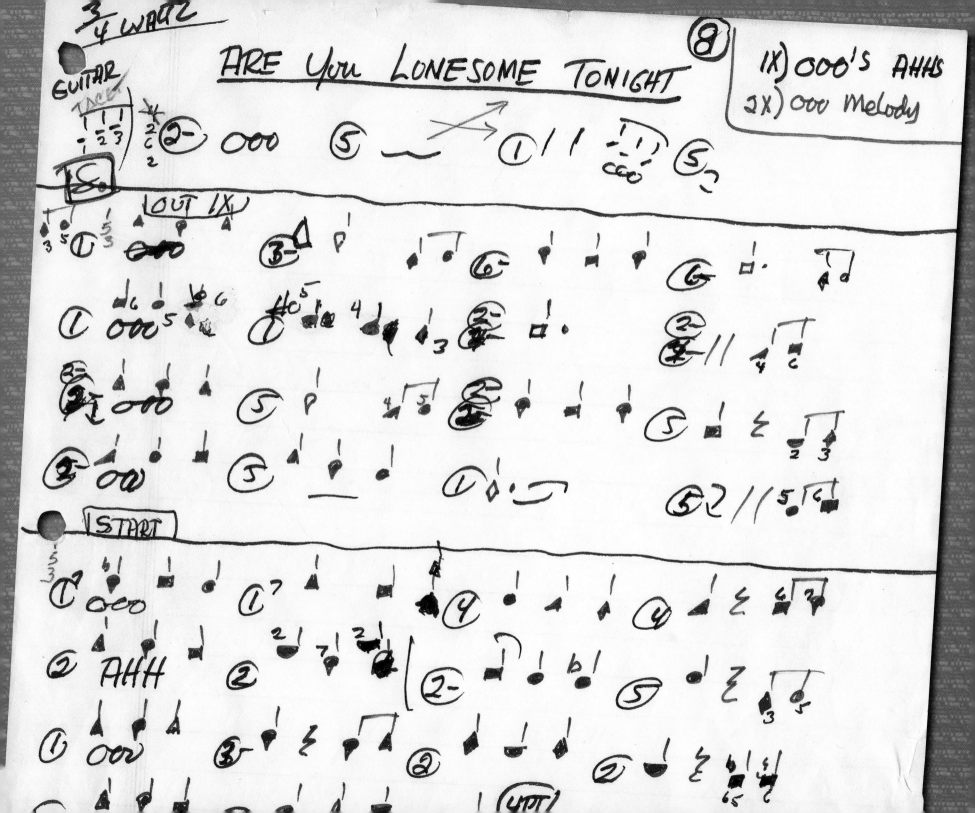

and, literally, within an arm's distance or less, was Colonel Parker, Steve Sholes, [another] VP from RCA, and Chet Atkins, all like—if I make a mistake, they're going to grab me, you know. They'd just [stand] there with this anticipation, 'Is it gonna happen?' After the first tune was done, they sat down. That's how much pressure was there on that first session. I'd been there just about a year, and I didn't have too much experience in the music business yet." Of the six songs Presley recorded that day, three made the pop charts. "Stuck on You" scrambled all the way to the peak of *Billboard*'s pop ranking, and its flip side, "Fame and Fortune," made it to #17.

Presley returned to Studio B a few weeks later, on April 3, 1960, for another all-night session. The twelve-hour marathon revealed Presley's growing confidence, subtlety, and vocal range, with "Reconsider Baby," a bluesy song featuring saxophonist Boots Randolph, and the sultry "Fever," a crossover hit for King Records R&B artist Little Willie John. Another timeless Presley performance from this session was the dramatic "It's Now or Never," with English lyrics set to the melody of the Italian standard "O Sole Mio."

Porter recalled this last recording vividly: "Elvis himself onstage said many times—I've heard him—that [it] was the biggest record he ever had, worldwide … We did multiple takes on that tune, and every time he got to the end, he'd crack that last note because it was out of his range. And he

Elvis with the Jordanaires, mid-1950s.
Left to right: Gordon Stoker, Hoyt Hawkins, Neal Matthews Jr., Hugh Jarrett.

# Special Delivery

Colonel Tom Parker, Elvis's manager, often leaked news to a DJ that Elvis was in town recording at Studio B. The DJ would tell listeners he heard that Elvis was at Studio B, and they would show up hoping to spot Elvis or, better yet, get an autograph. One day, a crowd gathered around the back door of Studio B, and I joined them to see if an Elvis sighting happened.

While we were waiting, I saw a delivery truck pull up by Studio B's front door. Not unusual. A delivery man got out of the truck wearing a uniform which included a hat. When a couple more delivery men got out of the truck and headed to Studio B's front door in a run, we realized the first uniformed delivery man was Elvis.

Of course, Parker staged the DJ tip and the delivery truck to promote Elvis.

– Ronny Light
RCA producer

kept doing it and doing it, and one time I remember pushing the talk-back button. I said, 'E.P., we can just do the ending. I can splice it on.'

"He said, 'Bill, I'm gonna do it all the way through, or I'm not gonna do it.'

"So we did it, and they got it. When I got through the session, and all the masters were ready to be played back, I played that tune back for him about eight times.

"He said, 'Bill, let me hear it again! Let me hear it again! Let me hear it again! Let me hear it again!'…When the bodyguards really heard it the second time, they all came in the studio and were just going crazy, slapped me on the back, 'Man, that's fantastic!' [They] were going nuts.

"Of course, he ate it up: 'Let me hear it again! Let me hear it again!'. . . He played the other tunes, too, but he wanted to hear that song over and over and over, almost to the point that the staff was coming in before he left to go home, eight o'clock the next morning. I think he would've probably heard it longer, but it was getting close to them coming to work, so he didn't want to be there then."

A #1 pop hit, "It's Now or Never" was another triumph for Presley, and so was a far different recording he made at that same session—the slow, sparely accompanied "Are You Lonesome Tonight?" For Porter, recording this theatrical Al Jolson number required quick thinking. "We had just done a tune of a pretty up tempo," he explained, "and I had a lot of echoes set up on the console. What I would normally do when we get through, I just feed the masters [controls] down and edit it off that tape and turn around and turn the masters back up on the console where we listed things. They would be preset [to] what I had last time, as far as echo was concerned and balances and so forth. And then, when they'd run through the [next] song, I'd be making these adjustments. Change the balance of the rhythm or change the echo sound, whatever.

"When I looked at the studio, the lights were off. Steve Sholes was sitting up there at the A&R position. I said, 'Mr. Sholes, I'm ready to listen.'

"He says, 'Roll the tape, Bill.'

"But then I said, 'I haven't heard the song.'

"'Roll the tape.'

"'Yes, sir.'"

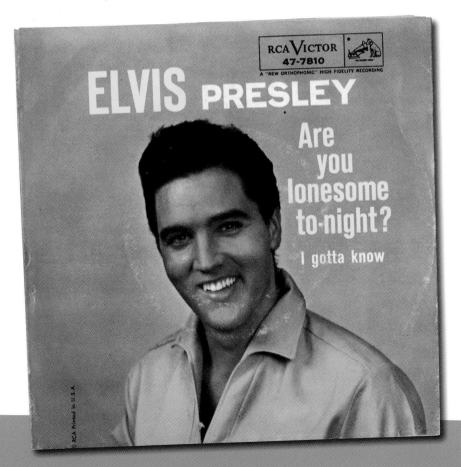

"So I rolled the tape, and I still can't see anything out there. After a few bars, I realized that we don't have a lot of people playing. There's no piano, and there's no electric guitar; it's just acoustic guitar and bass and the Jordanaires. So I'm turning a few mikes off to isolate things as much as I possibly can. All of a sudden Elvis starts talking. I thought, 'Uh-oh. All this echo—that ain't too good,' because it sounds like he's back in a cavern somewhere. I thought, 'Well, OK. Next take, I'll know where it comes. I'll turn it down.'

"Did the take all the way through. The Jordanaires made a mistake on the end, wrong chord. Started a second take. Got maybe, oh, one, two lines into it, and Elvis said, 'Hold it.' They stopped. He said, 'Mr. Sholes'— the light's still off in the studio—he said, 'I can't do this song justice. Throw it out.'

"Steve looked at me, he said, 'Don't you dare, Bill. That's a hit and I know it.' He pushed the talk-back button. He said, 'E.P., I'd like to get one good cut all the way through, if you don't mind, so we'll have it.' He said, 'Let's just do the ending where the Jordanaires made a mistake.'

"Elvis said, 'OK.'

"So they did just the ending. Couple chords back, you know. And then Steve looked at me. He said, 'Now, you splice that after I'm gone and send it to me tomorrow. 'I want you to use the first one as far as you possibly can, and just put the ending on.'

Cover for Presley's 1960 single "Are You Lonesome Tonight?" with B-side "I Gotta Know."

"Me being kind of stupid in those days, I did exactly what he said. I took it as far as I could, and 'to' was on one side of the splice, and 'night' is on the other! 'To-night!'" Only Porter knew this inside story, of course, and the public sent the hit straight up *Billboard*'s pop chart to #1.

On October 30, 1960, when Presley, his "Memphis Mafia" buddies, Tom Parker, and Hill and Range Songs rep Freddy Bienstock next appeared behind Studio B, the singer was in fine spirits, despite having to wear a bandage after breaking a finger during a touch football game. He was going to record a sacred album, a project he'd been excited about for a long time. *His Hand in Mine* reveals Presley at his best, voicing the spiritual core of his art. The collection includes Presley and the Jordanaires singing black religious songs such as "Joshua Fit the Battle," the Albert E. Brumley favorite "If We Never Meet Again," Stuart Hamblen's moving "Known Only to Him," and Artie Glenn's "Crying in the Chapel."

Ever versatile, at this same session Presley recorded the decidedly secular "Surrender," adapted from the Italian song "Come Back to Sorrento." Capturing the sexual attraction of lovers with hearts on fire, "Surrender" is essentially a song of seduction, yet Presley's rendition lightens the mood just enough to give the story a veneer of innocence. This release filled the #1 slot for two of the twelve weeks it spent on *Billboard*'s pop chart.

Above left: Cover for Presley's 1961 single "Lonely Man." The B-side, "Surrender," became the hit, rising to #1.

Left: *Billboard* Hot 100 chart for August 28, 1960, with "It's Now or Never" at #1. The hit remained at #1 for five of the twenty weeks it charted.

# Music City, USA

This Old House Is Still Swinging

**Bradley** RECORDING STUDIOS, Inc.

804 16th Avenue, South
Nashville 4, Tenn.

Following examples set by Decca in 1947 and RCA in 1955, other record labels established Nashville offices. In 1962, Capitol and ABC-Paramount created local outposts. In that same year, Columbia bought the Bradley Studios, built its Nashville headquarters around the legendary Quonset Hut, and, in short order, added another, larger studio. Warner Bros. and Sun were also active in Music City, as were Imperial and Mercury-Phillips-Smash, which signed singer-songwriter Roger Miller after RCA corporate bigwigs told Chet Atkins to let Miller go, in spite of his RCA hits "You Don't Want My Love" and "When Two Worlds Collide."

Above right: Early ad for Bradley Film and Recording Studios.

Right: Bradley Studios, 804 16th Avenue South, c. 1960. The Quonset Hut can be seen at the rear of the main building.

Groundbreaking for RCA Studio A, 1965.

We are Building . . .
NEW STUDIOS & OFFICE BUILDING FOR

RCA VICTOR
RECORD DIVISION

W. B. CAMBRON & COMPANY, INC.
GENERAL CONTRACTORS

(Both were recorded at Studio B during the years 1960 to 1961.) New studios sprang up to accommodate local sessions, which mushroomed from approximately 500 in 1957 to some 5,500 by 1968. A decade later, the city's total number of master and demo sessions approached 37,000 per year. In the early 1960s, Sun Records' Sam Phillips established a studio on Seventh Avenue North downtown, then sold it to Monument's Fred Foster. After selling their Music Row studios to Columbia, the Bradleys waited the contractually required three years, then opened Bradley's Barn, a new studio in nearby Wilson County, in 1965.

In early 1965, Chet Atkins and Owen Bradley opened a studio next door to Studio B and began renting it to RCA. Since this new facility was much larger than RCA's small studio at the corner of 17th Avenue South and Hawkins Street, the new studio became RCA Studio A, and the older, smaller studio became known as RCA Studio B. The Studio A building also housed a smaller recording space, designated Studio C. In 1961, RCA had built a smaller

Above right: Bobby Sykes recording with the Jordanaires, probably Bradley Studios, c. early 1960s. Left to right: Sykes, Ray Walker, soprano Millie Kirkham, Gordon Stoker, Neal Matthews, Hoyt Hawkins.

Right: Patti Page dancing at a session, Bradley Studios, c. 1961.

studio within the Studio B building, and used it mainly for mastering and lacquering discs before sending them to the label's various pressing plants. With the opening of Studios A and C, this older, smaller space was named Studio D.

Nevertheless, Studio B held its own, as even more studios came online during the late 1960s and 1970s. One-time Elvis Presley guitarist Scotty Moore began Music City Recorders in the mid-60s, and in 1967, Woodland Sound Studios opened across the Cumberland River in East Nashville. At about this same time, Acuff-Rose Publications built a studio in its new building on Franklin Road, and by the mid-1970s, Nashville studios included Quadrafonic (founded by bassist Norbert Putnam and keyboardist David Briggs), Mercury Custom Recording, DBM, Pete's Place (owned by steel guitarist and producer Pete Drake), and Wayne Moss's Cinderella Sound—among many more.

**TAPE PRICES**

| 3M TAPE TYPE | SIZE | LENGTH | PRICE |
|---|---|---|---|
| 131 | ¼" | 2400' | $10.00 |
| 131 | ½" | 2400' | 19.00 |
| 139 | ¼" | 2400' | 14.00 |
| 139 | ½" | 2400' | 25.00 |
| *111-A | ¼" | 1200' | 3.50 |
| *111-A | ¼" | 2500' | 7.00 |

*EXCELLENT FOR DEMO SESSIONS

THE WORLD'S MOST Know How and Finest Equipment in both STEREO and MONOPHONIC MASTERING. Stereo cut in both COMPATIBLE and REGULAR Stereophonic Ultra High-Fidelity

Note: All acetate dubs are cut to the same high standards as masters.

*The Sound of the Future Today in Nashville*

# SAM PHILLIPS
## RECORDING STUDIO
### OF NASHVILLE, INC.

319 7th AVE. NO.   PHONE AL 5-5424   NASHVILLE, TENN.

**FACILITIES — RATES**
**(Effective January 1, 1963)**

- Nashville's Largest & Finest
- Accoustically Unexcelled in U. S.
- Sound Versatility Unlimited
- Neuman — Ampex — Telefunken
- Custom Equipment Throughout
- Neuman's Biggest Lathe
- Nation's Finest Acetate Mastering & Dubbing Facilities
- Over 20 Years Experience

COMBINING NASHVILLE'S FABULOUSLY COMMERCIAL MUSICIANS WITH "MUSIC CITY'S" FINEST & MOST VERSATILE STUDIO IN A RELAXED ATMOSPHERE

FOR

**THE NASHVILLE SOUND**
**in the heart of**
**MUSIC CITY U.S.A.**

Above left: This sign was displayed for decades at Cinderella Sound, the Nashville studio owned and operated by guitarist Wayne Moss.
*Courtesy of Wayne Moss*

Left: Brochure from Sam Phillips Recording Studio of Nashville, Inc., early 1960s.
*Courtesy of the Sam Phillips family*

# Studio B and the Rise of Monument Records

After creating Monument Records and music publishing company Combine Music in Washington, D.C., in 1958, entrepreneur Fred Foster looked for a song he thought would excite the growing folk music market while also pleasing the general public. He found it in "Gotta Travel On," a public domain number on which he based a new arrangement. Foster had seen Atkins's ability to reach audiences at area clubs, and asked him to set up a Nashville session to record Billy Grammer's rendition of the song at Studio B late in 1958. In 1959 the release became a Top Five country hit while peaking at #4 on the pop charts. Foster soon moved

Left, Billy Grammer and Fred Foster, RCA Studio B, c. 1958.

Below: Grammer's 1959 hit album *Travelin' On.*

his recording and publishing operations to Nashville. "T for Texas," a #5 country chart hit for Monument's Grandpa Jones in 1963, was cut in Studio B, as was steel guitarist Jerry Byrd's "Theme from Adventures in Paradise," for an ABC-TV series that ran from 1959 until 1962.

Boots Randolph, whom Atkins brought to Nashville as a session player and recording artist, first recorded "Yakety Sax" for RCA, but he didn't sell strongly enough to suit RCA's New York decision makers, and on their directive, Atkins reluctantly dropped him. Randolph's Monument version of "Yakety Sax," was a Top Forty pop hit in 1963, and the number became his signature.

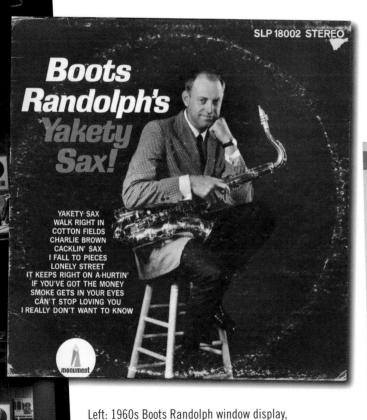

Left: *Boots Randolph's Yakety Sax!* (1963).

Below: Grandpa Jones's 1963 Monument album *Yodeling Hits.*

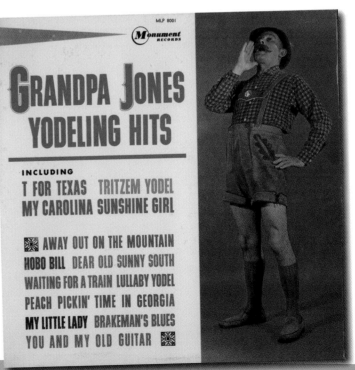

Left: 1960s Boots Randolph window display, reading "American Airlines Salute Monument Records and Boots Randolph."

# "Running Scared"

## By Bill Porter

### Former RCA Studio B Chief Engineer

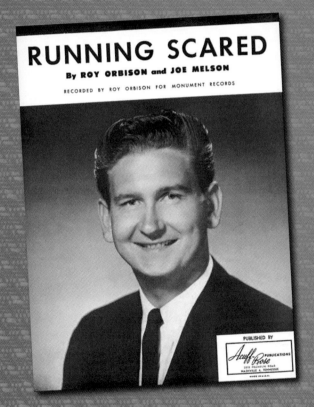

Sheet music for "Running Scared,"
Acuff-Rose Publications, Nashville, 1961.

On "Running Scared," Harold Bradley starts out playing the acoustic guitar in the intro. He didn't play it all the way through, because there was some discussion about trying to reinforce the sound. Harold really came in to play the electric bass guitar—not the electric bass, but electric bass guitar, that Danelectro, the clicking bass. [This is commonly known as the tick-tack bass guitar.] After the intro on the acoustic guitar, Harold puts the guitar down and walks about [six feet]. He picks up his electric [bass guitar] and gets ready, and he joins in on the song, but not at a place you would think. It's almost like in the middle of a bar. But it adds more emphasis to it and just builds. And his effect that he added gave it much more depth on the low end.

From the very beginning of the song to the very end, there's a twenty-five-decibel dynamic range. Now, classical music is about a forty in most cases. So we were approaching that, and that was kind of unheard of for a commercial 45-rpm [single]. In fact, people would say, "You can't do that." Well, I did it . . . But you've got to set those priorities and understand what's going to happen; you've got to start low and let it go high. If you start high [and] then [try to] go higher, you can't do it.

Roy Orbison session, Studio B, early 1960s.
Left to right: Hank Garland, Anita Kerr Singers (Kerr, Dottie Dillard, Louis Nunley),
Harold Bradley, Orbison (standing), James Wilkerson, Fred Foster.

Roy Orbison takes a break in Studio B, early 1960s.
*Photo by Elmer Williams*

# Roy Orbison
# Monument's Operatic Balladeer

Fred Foster achieved his greatest success with Texan Roy Orbison, whose lackluster sales on RCA led top-level bosses to trim him from their roster. Before Foster bought the Sam Phillips Studio in downtown Nashville in 1964, he and Orbison made a series of international pop hits at RCA Studio B, "Only the Lonely," "Blue Angel," "Running Scared," "Crying," and "In Dreams" among them.

Bill Porter relished his work with Orbison. Even on operatic ballads like these, Orbison's natural instinct was to sing softly, and the orchestral arrangements Foster commissioned tended to cover up his vocals. Lacking sophisticated electronic effects available today, Porter used the tools at hand. "Taking the three-track tape," he said, "which, his voice was on that [center] track by itself, I ran that track back into the console, which is like a feedback loop. But I fed just enough up into the mix that it would reinforce the sound and make it sound bigger."

The title track for this 1963 album features a unique, rhythmic string arrangement.

Porter had other ways of using echo to boost Orbison's vocal presence and give record buyers the sensation of being in a large performance venue. **He placed a speaker and a microphone in a room located just above the Studio B control room ceiling; this chamber had a highly reflective surface to make the sound from the speaker reverberate.** He then used the microphone to feed some of this sound back into the mixing board as recording took place; the split-second delay created the desired echo effect. During Porter's tenure as Studio B's chief engineer, from 1959 to 1963, the studio was equipped with German EMT echo devices consisting of metal plates, into which Porter routed the output signal to make the plates vibrate; as with the original echo chamber, he fed a portion of the resulting sound back into the mixing board. Porter learned to tighten the springs on the EMTs to heighten their vibrations, and to put them in a cold, air-conditioned room to make their metal plates ring.

Right: Speaker in echo chamber located above the Studio B control room.

*Photos by Bob Delevante*

Of all the Orbison recordings he engineered, Porter was proudest of "Running Scared." "That's a classical-type dynamic range," he stressed. "Dynamic range is the difference between the very softest note and the very loudest note. Of course, operatic music and classical music are known for having wide dynamic range, because it's real soft or it's real loud. This particular song, 'Running Scared,' started real soft and built and built and built as the arrangement went on and on and on, and I wanted to capture that sound so much. I changed my balance concept on that song about three different times trying to get [those] dynamics going. And it all happened."

Orbison's first #1 hit, "Running Scared" was one of his most stirring performances.

Left and right: Promotional photos of Roy Orbison, 1960s.

Below: Deagan vibraphone, heard on Orbison's 1960 hit "Only the Lonely."
*Photo by Bob Delevante*

# The Everly Brothers
## From Cadence to Warner Bros.

Don and Phil Everly, young men whose harmony enthralled millions of youthful fans in both pop and country markets, used RCA Studio B to record best-sellers for Archie Bleyer's New York–based Cadence label. In 1958 alone, the Everlys cut "All I Have to Do Is Dream," "Bird Dog," and "Devoted to You"—crossover hits penned by famed husband-wife songwriting team Boudleaux and Felice Bryant—each of which voiced the pangs and pleasures of teenagers falling in and out of love. After the Everlys' manager, Wesley Rose, switched them to Warner Bros., the brothers scored with numbers such as "Cathy's Clown," "Ebony Eyes," "Walk Right Back," and "Crying in the Rain," all pop hits recorded at Studio B in the years from 1960 to 1962.

The Everly Brothers (Don at left), recording in RCA Studio B, c. 1958.
*Photo by Elmer Williams*

Left to right: Phil Everly, Wesley Rose,
Boudleaux Bryant, Don Everly, Studio B, c. 1960.
*Photo by Elmer Williams*

# "Take a Message"

At the session when they were recording "Take a Message to Mary," [Cadence Records producer] Archie Bleyer said to Boudleaux, "You know, I hear a *chink, chink, chink* in this [song]... Somebody get me a Coke bottle, and somebody get me a screwdriver... Here, Boudleaux, you belong to the [musicians] union. Hit this Coke bottle, and that'll take care of what I think I hear." So that's what you hear on the Everlys' record of "Take a Message to Mary." You hear Boudleaux playing a Coke bottle!

– Felice Bryant
   Co-writer, "Take a Message to Mary"

Above right: Radio station WMAK, Nashville, c. 1960.
Standing: Don Everly, radio host Ralph Emery, unidentified, Phil Everly. Seated: Unidentified, disc jockey Bill Morgan.

Right: Boudleaux and Felice Bryant, c. 1960.

*Photos by Elmer Williams*

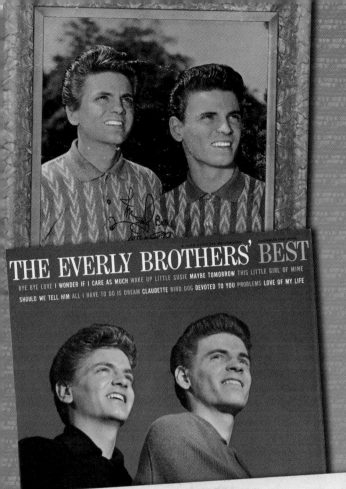

# "Those were fun sessions"

## By Ray Edenton
### Guitarist

Those were fun sessions. Don made the arrangements, and he led the sessions playing strong rhythm guitar in an open tuning, so he could play a chord simply by strumming and using one finger of his left hand to fret the strings all the way across the guitar neck. At first I doubled him on an arch-top Gibson guitar in standard tuning, so I was making chords with however many fingers I needed. Later, I matched Don using a flat-top Martin.

Phil and Don had that great, close country harmony that only two brothers or sisters can make. And they brought that harmony right into the rock and roll era with strong rhythm guitar playing. Plus, their material appealed to both young adults and teenaged kids, because love is something everybody can relate to.

Left, top to bottom: *A Date with the Everly Brothers* (released 1960, pictured 1962 cover), *The Everly Brothers' Best* (1959), *The Fabulous Style of the Everly Brothers* (1960).

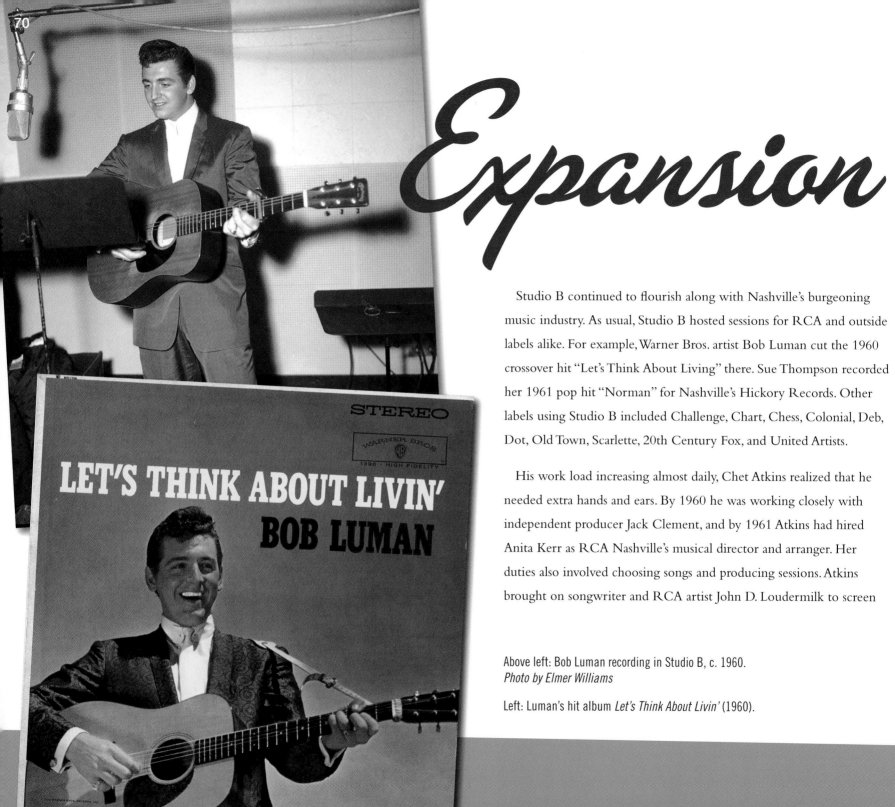

# Expansion

Studio B continued to flourish along with Nashville's burgeoning music industry. As usual, Studio B hosted sessions for RCA and outside labels alike. For example, Warner Bros. artist Bob Luman cut the 1960 crossover hit "Let's Think About Living" there. Sue Thompson recorded her 1961 pop hit "Norman" for Nashville's Hickory Records. Other labels using Studio B included Challenge, Chart, Chess, Colonial, Deb, Dot, Old Town, Scarlette, 20th Century Fox, and United Artists.

His work load increasing almost daily, Chet Atkins realized that he needed extra hands and ears. By 1960 he was working closely with independent producer Jack Clement, and by 1961 Atkins had hired Anita Kerr as RCA Nashville's musical director and arranger. Her duties also involved choosing songs and producing sessions. Atkins brought on songwriter and RCA artist John D. Loudermilk to screen

Above left: Bob Luman recording in Studio B, c. 1960.
*Photo by Elmer Williams*

Left: Luman's hit album *Let's Think About Livin'* (1960).

song material and produce certain artists. "When it came to hunting for songs," Loudermilk said, "Chet told us, 'Listen to the first song on each tape. Don't listen to it twice; don't listen to the second one. Everybody puts the best song on the very first one. If they don't know that they need to fail.' He also told us to look for tape boxes that were decorated. 'This could be a sign of commerciality,' he said."

In addition to Atkins, by June 1962 RCA's Nashville staff counted Ed Hines, head of custom (non-RCA) recording; radio and TV promoter Bob Holt; recorded program service director Jack Deal; and administrative assistants Juanita Jones, Mrs. Eddie Jackson, Ina Harris, and Polly Roper. Three engineers—Bill Porter, Tommy Strong, and Bill Vandervort— manned the technical aspects of recording. Others who would serve as engineers included George Bennett, Roy Butts, Milton Henderson, Randy Kling, Les Ladd, and Jim Malloy, along with Al Pachucki, Tom Pick, Bill Rosee, Dave Roys, Mike Shockley, Roy Shockley, Chuck Seitz, and Ron Steele.

Above right: Chet Atkins and Anita Kerr studying session charts, c. 1961.

Right: Frances Preston, head of BMI Nashville, Jack Clement, and Juanita Jones, of ASCAP, at the opening of Clement's Nashville studio, 1969.

# *Hit* Factory

As the 1960s progressed, RCA's Nashville-based artists created hit after hit in Studio B. Gravel-voiced Hank Snow reached #1 in 1962 with "I've Been Everywhere." On Skeeter Davis's "The End of the World" which peaked at #2 on the country and pop charts in 1963, studio musicians supported her plaintive country vocals with piano arpeggios, strings, and a hint of steel guitar. Davis sang her own vocal harmony, and added a speaking part. "That's the one that she overdubbed the vocal part on, the dialogue," Bill Porter recalled. "Skeeter reminded me that that was kind of an afterthought, to do the dialogue. So they called me at home, asked me would I come back to the studio the next day because they wanted to do the overdub."

Above right: Hank Snow's 1963 album *I've Been Everywhere.*

Right: Snow in Studio B, 1962.
*Courtesy of Sony Music Archives*

Skeeter Davis and Bobby Bare in Studio B, c. 1965.
*Courtesy of Sony Music Archives*

Porter Wagoner, a dyed-in-the-wool RCA country singer from West Plains, Missouri, joined the Grand Ole Opry in 1957, and began starring in his own syndicated TV show in 1961. The program gave him weekly exposure in eighty markets by 1965, and one hundred markets by 1970, thereby boosting record sales and drawing larger crowds on the road. Wagoner's passion for bright colors and Nudie suits decorated with sequins, rhinestones, and fancy embroidery helped him connect with audiences on hits such as 1962's "Misery Loves Company"; 1965's "Green, Green Grass of Home"; 1967's "The Cold Hard Facts of Life," and other straight-country fare. Chet Atkins or, later, RCA staff producer Bob Ferguson, was typically on hand, but Wagoner virtually produced his own sessions. W Wagoner agoner recorded with the Blackwood Brothers in Studio B, winning three Grammys for their efforts in 1966, 1967, and 1969.

Likewise, pop-leaning RCA country acts kept delivering the goods. In December 1963, Dottie West and Jim Reeves cut the Top Ten country duet "Love Is No Excuse." With her song "Here Comes My Baby," co-written with first husband Bill West and recorded in Studio B in 1964, West won the first Grammy ever awarded for Best Country Vocal Performance, Female.

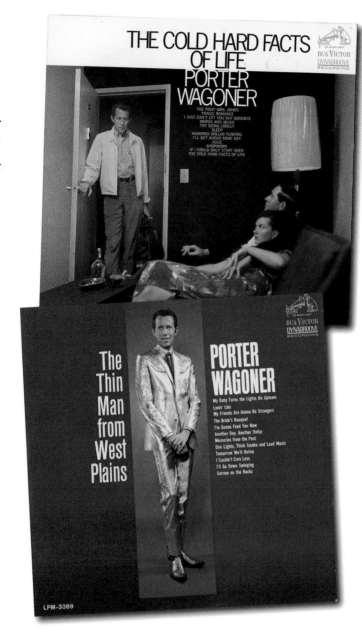

Far left: Dottie West's breakthrough album, *Here Comes My Baby* (1965).

Left: West in the studio, 1965. *Courtesy of Sony Music Archives*

Above: Covers for Porter Wagoner's *The Cold Hard Facts of Life* (1967) and *The Thin Man from West Plains* (1965).

Crossover artist Jim Reeves remained a powerful chart presence well past his untimely death in a 1964 plane crash. In addition to his duet with Dottie West, hits he cut in Studio B include "I Know One," a second version of "Am I Losing You," "The Blizzard," and "Welcome to My World." "Jim had a perfect recording voice," Reeves's former business partner Tom Perryman said. "That's the main reason the records he made before the crash kept charting after he died." "I Guess I'm Crazy," "This Is It," and "Is It Really Over?"—the last featuring the mellow trombone of Nashville Symphony member Gene Mullins—made it to #1 during 1964 and 1965, and from 1968 to 1970 Reeves was never out of the Top Ten. RCA continued to release the singer's recordings into the 1980s. Before his passing, overseas tours and international marketing had grown his worldwide following to enormous proportions. A Jim Reeves cult developed in the Caribbean and in Africa, and as late as 1982 some West African fans insisted that he was not a man, but an angel.

After a sales slump in the late 1950s and early 1960s, Eddy Arnold began a comeback that amounted to a second career. He did see chart action with Jimmie Driftwood's "Tennessee Stud" and he scored other Top Ten hits, but sales were modest until 1965's "What's He Doing in My World," from a January 1965 Studio B session, went to #1. Arnold's massive 1965 crossover hit "Make the World Go Away" (#1 country, #6 pop) was among the first recordings made in the newer Studio A.

Above left: This 1962 album showed Jim Reeves's cosmopolitan image.

Left to right: Jim Reeves, Bobby Bare, Anita Kerr, and Chet Atkins at JFK International Airport, April 1964.
*Courtesy of Sony Music Archives*

Clean-cut, mellow-voiced George Hamilton IV, having converted to country music after his breakthrough 1956 pop hit "A Rose and a Baby Ruth," asked Chet Atkins to record him, and after three Top Ten hits in 1961 and 1962, his rendition of "Abilene" went #1 country and #15 pop in 1963. "Abilene" and other RCA hits endeared Hamilton to audiences in Canada, Great Britain, Europe, and Russia, earning him the name Country Music's Ambassador.

Bobby Bare also sought Atkins's favor, and made his first RCA sides in Studio B in 1962. A native of Ironton, Ohio, Bare had a #2 pop hit in 1959 with "The All American Boy," issued on Fraternity Records under songwriter Bill Parsons's name because Bare, the real vocalist, was in military service and couldn't tour. (On the road, Parsons lip-synched to a recording of Bare's voice.) When Bare approached Atkins, he was eager to establish his own artistic identity.

**"I was full of piss and vinegar back then," Bare said. "So I told Chet, 'I know I can cut hits.' Fortunately, he gave me a chance, and in 1962 I had 'Shame on Me,' which went to #23 on the pop chart."**

In 1963 Bare recorded the Grammy-winning "Detroit City," a Danny Dill–Mel Tillis song earlier recorded by Monument's Billy Grammer (as "I Wanna Go Home"). "Grammer came up with turning the low E string of [an acoustic] guitar down to D," Bare explained. "When I did it, it was strictly Chet's idea to use an electric guitar

Top to Bottom: Three powerhouse RCA albums: Eddy Arnold's *My World* (1965), George Hamilton IV's *Abilene* (1963), and Bobby Bare's *500 Miles Away from Home* (1963).

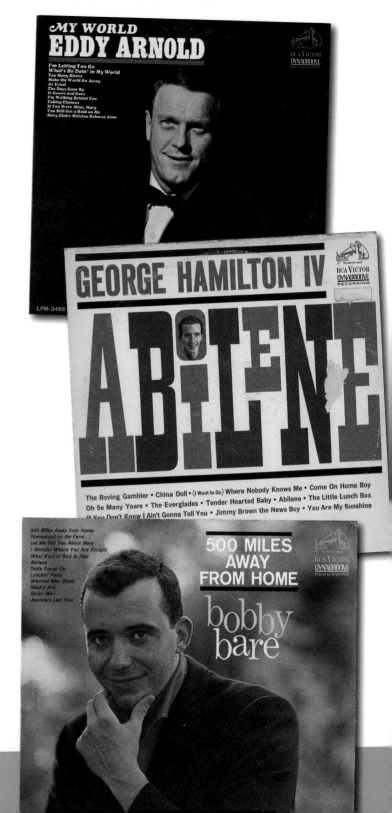

When I walked in Studio B to record my recent album *Darker than Light*, I saw my career. Everywhere I looked, I saw Chet Atkins, Floyd Cramer, all of 'em. Being there and seeing all these great talented people in my mind had a real effect on me. It was like a trip back to the time I recorded hits there. It was an inspiration to me and to the younger musicians who played on the album.

—Bobby Bare

for this effect." In 1963 and 1964, Bare compiled three straight crossover hits—"Detroit City" (#6 country, #16 pop), "500 Miles Away from Home" (#5 country, #10 pop), and the haunting story song "Miller's Cave" (#4 country, #33 pop).

"Bobby had a great talent," Bill Porter said. "He didn't get into a lot of multiple takes. He got things together, and he talked on those songs, and these were not overdubs. He just leaned into the microphone when he wanted to talk, and, of course, I turned everything else down so you could really hear it. Nowadays, it's an easy thing to do; you overdub it, and that's it. But it was all done live, and he did a fantastic job. His interpretation, musically, was phenomenal."

Freelance producer Jack Clement oversaw the recordings that brought Charley Pride to Chet Atkins's attention in 1965. Steel guitar player Lloyd Green remembered making these in Clement's Nashville studio, and liking what he heard: "Cowboy Clement produced Charley in a split session," Green said. "He recorded two songs with Charley, and two he sang himself. I really liked Charley's voice; it was really, really good. It was basically smooth, but it still had an edge to it." Amid the racial tensions of the 1960s, top RCA executives were

Above left: Bobby Bare, c. 1964.

Right: Album cover for *Detroit City and Other Hits by Bobby Bare* (1963).

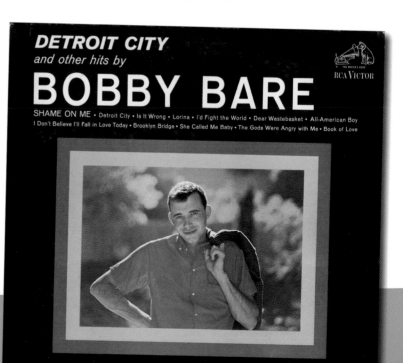

wary of signing an African-American country singer, but Atkins persuaded them to give Pride a chance to prove himself. Pride did just that: Over the next two decades, fifty-one Top Ten RCA hits, including twenty-nine #1s, made Pride one of the most successful artists ever to cut a country disc—in Studio B or anywhere else. "From 'The Snakes Crawl at Night,' one of his first releases, to 'Just Between You and Me,' his first Top Ten, and hits like "Is Anybody Goin' to San Antone' and 'Kiss an Angel Good Morning' in the early 1970s," Green said, "I recorded all of Charley's early hits with him in Studio B. He was great to record with, because he sang so well. And he took to me right from the start. He loved the musical ideas I came up with to complement his singing. One time he came over and touched my head and said, 'Take care of that great brain.'

"As a studio musician," Green stressed, "I liked everything about Studio B—the acoustics, the feel, the layout. It was like home. It had a certain amount of love, comfort—something special. Also, I loved the engineers. Al Pachucki loved the steel guitar, and he was a steel player's dream when it came to engineering. Chuck Seitz [and] Bill Vandervort were good, too. So many artists made their first hits there—not just Charley, but Lynn Anderson, for example. She recorded "Ride, Ride, Ride" and other hits for Chart Records at RCA B."

Above right: Charley Pride in Studio B, late 1960s.
*Courtesy of Sony Music Archives*

Right: Pride's 1967 albums
*Pride of Country Music* and *The Country Way*.

Always mindful of rising talent, Chet Atkins signed guitar slinger Jerry Reed to RCA in 1964. Reed was soon working as a studio musician as well as an artist, and Atkins admired his ability to add innovative licks that built upon what Atkins himself had come up with. Atkins also encouraged Reed to push beyond the boundaries of his own early work. As Reed put it, "One day Chet said, 'You should quit recording that way, because that ain't the way you feel. That ain't the way you are. The way you are is the way you are at my house when you get the guitar and play your licks and sing your songs.'" "Guitar Man" (1967) announced Reed's new approach, and he broke through with the crossover hits "Amos Moses" (1970) and "When You're Hot, You're Hot" (1971). All three numbers were cut in Studio B.

Top Left: Jerry Reed's *Nashville Underground* (1968).

Left and below: Reed in the studio, late 1960s.
*Photos courtesy of Sony Music Archives*

# "The Great Wall of Dolly"

Porter Wagoner and Dolly Parton, *Just Between You and Me* (1968).

## By Dolly Parton
### Member, Country Music Hall of Fame

I never was much of a driver, but I was on my way to the studio, and I was so excited. It was my first big deal with Porter [Wagoner], to record. I ran into the building out here—smashed the car into the building. But I didn't want to be late, so I just cut the ignition off, and bricks and things kind of scattered. Later on, when we finished the [session], people said, "Hey! Somebody ran into the building!" I called my father-in-law to come and get the car and take me home and send the car to the garage. After that, all the musicians and Chet Atkins and all the people, they referred to it as the Great Wall of Dolly.

Wagoner and Parton in Studio B's
"sweet spot," late 1960s.

Chet Atkins (left) and Waylon Jennings
in Atkins's home studio, late 1960s.

# RCA *Staff Producers*

So successful were RCA's Nashville artists that in 1968 the label made Atkins a company vice president. By this time, additional staff producers were sharing his load. Felton Jarvis joined in 1965 and began producing Elvis Presley. Among the other artists Jarvis supervised was singer-songwriter John Hartford, who recorded his Grammy-winning "Gentle on My Mind" at Studio B in 1967. Through recordings of the song by other singers including Glen Campbell, and Hartford's regular appearances opening CBS's *Glen Campbell Goodtime Hour*, "Gentle on My Mind" became one of the twentieth century's most-performed songs. Another singer-songwriter who recorded under Jarvis's direction was the widely respected Mickey Newbury. Newbury's original songs were covered by such artists as the First Edition ("Just Dropped In to See What Condition My Condition Was In"), Presley ("American Trilogy"), and Willie Nelson ("Sweet Memories").

Manuscript for John Hartford's "Gentle on My Mind," c. 1967.

One of producer Bob Ferguson's first assignments after signing on with RCA in the mid-1960s was working with Connie Smith, best known for her #1 hit "Once a Day." Artist and producer quickly bonded. "Bob was great about taking suggestions from everyone," Smith said, "and I helped him find songs, decide which ones to record, and choose musicians. I loved Weldon Myrick's steel-guitar playing, and you could say he became my dancing partner. He'd lead me into my vocal parts, and then make his own contributions. Bob even adjusted Weldon's amp by making it more treble. He said that treble sounds cut through on AM radio. We all enjoyed what we were doing and enjoyed each other. We worked as a group to make the music fit each song. With real creativity, you can direct it, but you can't control it. You've got to let it be and let it grow. It's all about communicating emotions."

Additionally, Ferguson was responsible for producing Porter Wagoner, as a solo artist and as a duo with Dolly Parton, who became the "girl singer" in Wagoner's band after he recruited her for the role in 1967. At the time, she was signed to Fred Foster's Monument label, and she remained grateful for his early support. ("Fred believed in me when no one else did," she said later.) But the opportunity to join Wagoner's troupe and reach large TV audiences was too great to pass up, and Foster let her go with his blessing. Studio B sessions yielded a string of duet hits that earned the pair honors as CMA's 1968 Vocal Group of the Year, and Vocal Group or Duo of the Year in 1970 and 1971.

The facility also saw the creation of solo hits such as Parton's "Just Because I'm a Woman," "Coat of Many Colors," and "Joshua," her first #1. Likewise, Wagoner lengthened his list of hit singles there with "Your Old Love Letters," "Cold Dark Waters," "Sorrow on the Rocks," "Skid Row Joe," "The Carroll County Accident" (a Ferguson original), and "Big Wind."

Far left: Connie Smith session at Studio B, late 1960s.
*Courtesy of Sony Music Archives*

Left to right: Album covers for Connie Smith's *Connie Smith* (1965) and *Cute 'n' Country* (1965).

Waylon Jennings in Studio B, c. 1967.
*Courtesy of Sony Music Archives*

Above: Porter Wagoner and Dolly Parton, c. 1967.
*Courtesy of Sony Music Archives*

Left: Dolly Parton's *Just Because I'm a Woman* (1968).

Danny Davis and the Nashville Brass, Jim Ed Brown, and Atkins himself were all under Ferguson's wing in the studio. Davis served as an RCA staff producer from 1965 to 1970, operating independently thereafter.

Ronny Light produced Waylon Jennings after the temperamental star's drug use—and clashes over Jennings's guitar playing—exhausted Davis's patience. Light had no problems with Jennings, and, depending on which room was available, used both Studio B and Studio A to produce popular recordings such as the 1972 album *Ladies Love Outlaws*. Light also produced Kenny Price, who made Top Ten hits in 1970 and 1971

with "Biloxi" and "The Sherriff of Boone County." With Atkins, Light coproduced Liz Anderson, Skeeter Davis, Dallas Frazier, Red Lane, and Tony Joe White, all in B, the studio that came to be known as "Little Victor."

Owen Bradley's son, Jerry, whom Atkins made his assistant in 1970, preferred the quiet "dead" environment of Studio A to Studio B's live, highly reflective sound, but he did produce Studio B sessions with Nat Stuckey, yielding 1973's "Take Time to Love Her," among other successful discs.

# Pop, Jazz, Gospel, and Bluegrass *at Studio B*

In addition to recordings by country performers, Studio B witnessed sessions by pop and jazz artists who availed themselves of RCA Nashville's excellent engineers and the city's growing cadre of inventive session musicians. Next to Elvis Presley, the most successful pop act to use the studio in the early 1960s was Roy Orbison, who did not chart country until 1980.

Fresh-faced teen idol Johnny Tillotson recorded for Cadence at Studio B. Among the songs he cut there was the 1960 #2 pop hit "Poetry in Motion"—the highest chart record he achieved. Swedish actress and pop singer Ann-Margret, then signed to RCA, cut her most successful chart record, "I Just Don't Understand," in 1961. (Fifty years later, first-call session players still remembered the sensation she caused by showing up wearing a leotard.) Also in 1961, African-American pop singer Robert Knight—later renowned for his 1967 pop hit

Rock & roll pioneer Esquerita in Studio B in 1958
with Capitol producer Ken Nelson.
*Photo by Elmer Williams*

Johnny Tillotson recording session in Studio B, c. 1960.
*Photo by Elmer Williams*

"Everlasting Love"—recorded "Because" for Dot. Rosemary Clooney made her biggest hits for Columbia, but she recorded country standards for her RCA album *Rosemary Clooney Sings Country Hits from the Heart* in Studio B sessions held in 1961 and 1962.

Bobby Goldsboro, who bridged pop and country audiences, used Studio B to record the 1968 international hit "Honey" for United Artists. Engineer Bill Vandervort remembered the technical difficulty involved: "The interesting thing about Bobby Goldsboro, 'Honey,' when he recorded that we had the old console, you know, twelve [inputs]. Of course, it was a big session with voices, strings, and percussion . . . and everything [was] live, and they didn't have enough inputs to mike everything. So the guy [engineer] who was normally helping the engineer [who ran] the tape machine in the control room had to go out with a hand mike and run around to the various instruments. If the percussionist was playing, he had to hold the mike on him as he

Left: Perry Como and Ray Edenton (in foreground) in Studio B, 1965. *Courtesy of Sony Music Archives*

Above: Among the songs RCA pop star Perry Como cut in Studio B were Willie Nelson's "My Own Peculiar Way," and "Dream on Little Dreamer" by Fred Burch and Jan Crutchfield.

Below, left to right: *Rosemary Clooney Sings Country Hits from the Heart* (1963), *Andy and the Bey Sisters* (1961), Al Hirt's *Honey in the Horn* (1963).

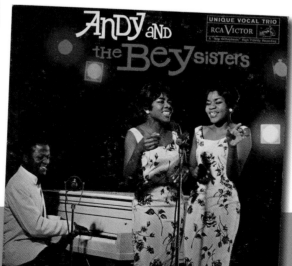

---

played, you see, and then he'd move on to the next instrument as *he* played." Reportedly selling more than five million copies, "Honey" conquered *Billboard*'s country and pop charts alike.

African-American jazz vocalists Andy Bey and his sisters Geraldine and Salome recorded at Studio B in the early 1960s. Jazz trumpeter Al Hirt, an RCA act, came to Nashville to make his critically acclaimed 1963 album *Honey in the Horn*. "Java," a single from this collection, went #4 pop in 1964.

Gospel acts had been recording for RCA in Nashville well before Studio B opened. The Blackwood Brothers, whose Memphis performances inspired Elvis Presley, recorded at the Methodist Television, Radio, and Film Commission studio as early as June 1957. Both the Blackwoods and the Statesmen frequented Studio B into the 1960s. In addition, Bill Porter remembered Studio B sessions with the Florida Boys, the Speer Family, the Oak Ridge Quartet (predecessor to the Oak Ridge Boys), and the

Cathedrals—all among gospel music's most recognized groups. Most RCA country acts of the day, and some signed to other labels, recorded gospel and Christmas albums there. Elvis Presley singles such as "Crying in the Chapel" and gospel albums including *His Hand in Mine*, also made in Studio B, found favor with country and pop listeners as well as with more specialized gospel audiences.

RCA lagged behind other labels in signing bluegrass bands, perhaps because the bluegrass market was relatively small. Nevertheless, West Coast country star Rose Maddox made her historic Capitol album *Rose Maddox Sings Bluegrass* in Studio B in 1962, coached by bluegrass progenitor Bill Monroe. After Lester Flatt and Earl Scruggs parted ways in 1969 and Flatt signed with RCA in 1971, he recorded primarily at Studio B with his band, the Nashville Grass. In early 1971, Flatt began recording at the studio with roots-music stalwart Mac Wiseman, and the pair completed three albums together.

Below, left to right: The Statesmen Quartet's *The Bible Told Me So* (1958), Elvis Presley's *His Hand in Mine* (1960), Porter Wagoner and the Blackwood Brothers Quartet's *The Grand Old Gospel* (1966).

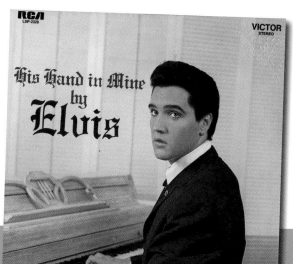

# King's Playground
## Elvis in Studio B, 1961–1971

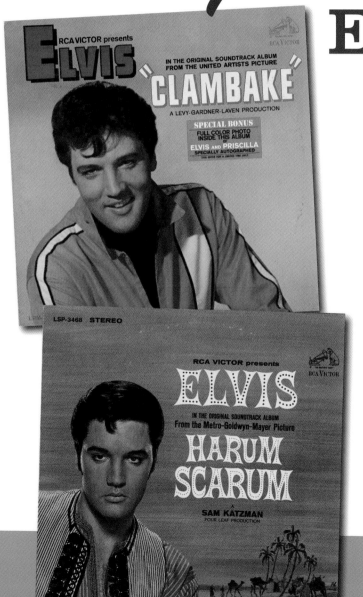

As Elvis Presley's career continued, he made many of his recordings in Hollywood or Memphis, but he returned often to RCA Studio B between 1961 and 1971. Over the course of this decade, his Studio B sessions yielded hit singles, a number of albums, and all or parts of five motion picture soundtracks: *Follow That Dream* (1962), *Kissin' Cousins* (1964), *Harum Scarum* (1965), *Clambake*—featuring Jerry Reed's "Guitar Man"—(1967), and *Stay Away Joe* (1968).

Along with movie soundtrack albums, other Presley collections and include songs recorded at Studio B are *Something for Everybody* (1961), *Pot Luck* (1962), and the gospel album *How Great Thou Art* (1967), the last containing "In the Garden," "Farther Along," and the stirring "Run On." Still other albums featuring Studio B–recorded cuts are *Elvis Country* (1971), *Elvis Now* (1972), *That's the Way It Is* (1971), *Love Letters from Elvis* (1970), and *Elvis Sings the Wonderful World of Christmas* (1971).

Sountracks to *Clambake* and *Harum Scarum*.

The decade 1961 to 1971 also saw Presley create some excellent hit singles in Studio B: the twin-sided chartmaker "(Marie's the Name) His Latest Flame" and "Little Sister," "She's Not You," "(You're the) Devil in Disguise," and "Crying in the Chapel." Others include "Indescribably Blue" (showcasing Harold Bradley's artful guitar work), the Jerry Reed compositions "Guitar Man" and "U.S. Male," "Big Boss Man," "You Don't Have to Say You Love Me," and "I Really Don't Want to Know." Although it was not a single, Presley recorded the concert favorite "My Way" in 1971; it was included in the 1995 collection *Walk a Mile in My Shoes: The Essential Seventies Masters.*

Above: At a 1971 recording session in Studio B.
Top row, L-R: Jerry Carrigan, drums; Al Pachucki, engineer; Elvis Presley; Norbert Putnam, bass; David Briggs, piano. Bottom row, L-R: James Burton, guitar; Charlie McCoy, harmonica; Jerry Stembridge, guitar; Felton Jarvis, producer.

Right: Studio B's celeste, c. early 1950s, can be heard on recordings such as Elvis Presley's "That's Someone You Never Forget" and "Winter Wonderland."

# Changing of the Guard

By 1973, Chet Atkins was growing weary of producing and attending to administrative details. "What makes being an A&R man so stressful," he told Lewis Anderson in 1992, "is having to say no . . . You gotta drop artists or sign artists, and tell a writer you can't use his song. It really tore my heart out to do that." Atkins had always felt more loyal to his mentor, Steve Sholes, than to RCA, and with Sholes's death, in 1968, Atkins no longer had a strong advocate within the corporation. Owen Bradley's son, Jerry, became RCA Nashville's executive producer in 1970, and succeeded Atkins as head of RCA Nashville in 1973—the year Atkins underwent successful surgery for colon cancer.

Above right: Chet Atkins and friend, c. 1975. RCA secured the rights to the famous Nipper logo when it acquired the Victor Talking Machine Company in 1929.
*Courtesy of Merle Atkins Russell and the Estate of Chester B. Atkins*

Right: Waylon Jennings and Jerry Bradley hold a framed gold record award for Jennings's 1978 album *I've Always Been Crazy*.

Atkins continued to record his own albums, and he retained the title of vice president until leaving RCA in 1982. He also produced a select number of artists, including Steve Wariner, then at the outset of his success. "I was playing bass for Bob Luman on the road and writing a lot of songs," Wariner said. "Johnny Cash was producing an album on Bob at the House of Cash studio in Hendersonville, Tennessee. I had four songs on the album. Guitarist Paul Yandell, a close friend of Chet's, was on one of the sessions, and asked me for a cassette to take to him. Chet then called me and wanted to hear more of my songs, and we set up a meeting at Studio B. When I came in the back door, Chet was at the console with an engineer, finishing up a Jerry Reed session. Chet introduced me to Jerry, and asked me to play "I'm Already Taken." After I did, Jerry said, "Damn, Chet! Sign this boy! What do you want, blood?" All of my RCA sessions were held in Studio A, but Studio B was where I got started with the label. It will always be special to me."

Top left: Playing bass, Steve Wariner backs Chet Atkins, c. 1983. *Photo by Theresa Montgomery*

Left, L-R: Bobby Bare, Jerry Reed, and Dickey Lee backstage during Fan Fair, c. 1975.

# *Outlaws* and Beyond

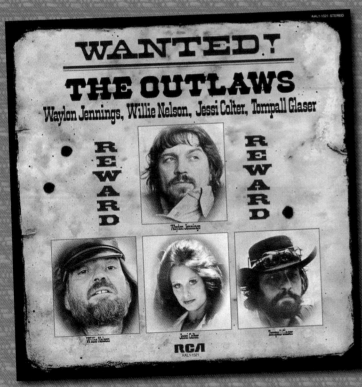

In 1975, Willie Nelson's self-produced Columbia album *Red Headed Stranger* won plaudits for its arrangements, which stood in contrast to the lush backgrounds of his 1960s RCA recordings made in Studio B. Some critics claimed that RCA had hindered Nelson's creativity through formulaic, pop-oriented arrangements. Atkins, while not endorsing this view, shared Nelson's frustration that the label often failed to promote Nashville product. Studio musicians later sounded a note of caution, though, pointing out that Nelson did record successful chart-making singles and albums for RCA. Moreover, they argued, Nelson sometimes recorded wearing a sport coat and tie during his Nashville years and didn't adopt his hip persona and stripped-down musical approach until he moved back to his native Texas in 1970.

Left: Album cover for *Wanted! The Outlaws* (RCA, 1976).

Opposite: Receiving awards for *Wanted! The Outlaws*. Back row, L-R: Tompall Glaser, RCA Records president Ken Glancy, RCA Nashville president Jerry Bradley, RCA VP Chet Atkins. Front row, L-R: Waylon Jennings, Jessi Colter, Willie Nelson.
*Courtesy of Sony Music Archives*

During the mid-1970s "Outlaw" years, Jennings's publicists cast him as a rebel fighting RCA's Nashville establishment. In truth, the company stayed with Jennings despite his erratic studio behavior and problems with substance abuse. RCA gave him advances against future royalties and financed his tours. Hits recorded at RCA Studio B during the late 1960s and early 1970s, such as "Stop the World and Let Me Off" and "Only Daddy That'll Walk the Line" helped to keep Jennings on the label. "We believed in Waylon as an artist," said RCA director of Nashville operations Joe Galante in 1986. (Galante joined the Nashville staff as manager of administration in 1973. He kept close tabs on the budget.) "So we hung in there with him. By 1976, when we released the *Outlaws* album, he was deep in the red in his account with us. Most labels wouldn't go that far with an artist today." In that year, RCA's faith paid off in the form of *Wanted! The Outlaws*, a repackaged set of recordings by Jennings, Nelson, Jessi Colter, and Tompall Glaser. Some of the songs had been cut in Studio B, and RCA engineer Bill Harris used the studio to remix the selections requested by Jerry Bradley. "On 'Good-Hearted Woman,'" Harris said, "Willie came in and overdubbed his part, which was combined with a version Waylon had

Top right: Chet Atkins, Waylon Jennings, and Willie Nelson, 1977.
*Photo by Les Leverett*

Right: Johnny Paycheck recording in Studio B, c. 1966.

already made." Glaser had gained visibility with "Put Another Log on the Fire" in 1975, and Jerry Bradley leased the master from Polydor. The album's popularity exploded—it eventually sold more than two million copies. Winning new fans for country music among college-age listeners, it became the first country album to be certified platinum by the Recording Industry Association of America (RIAA) for sales of a million copies.

Far from standing in Jennings's way, RCA Nashville chief Jerry Bradley conceived the idea for the project. "Hazel Smith, a local publicist, had already come up with the term 'outlaw,'" Bradley said, "and Time-Life was publishing a set of books in its Old West series. Each book was about a different topic, but all of them had similar covers with the look of hand-tooled leather. This was our inspiration for the 'wanted' poster we used for the cover of the *Outlaws* album. We put Willie, Waylon, Tompall, and Jessi on the poster as the outlaws the sheriffs were pursuing."

Publicists and music journalists burnished the singers' images as independent-minded singers who refused to compromise their artistic visions, and each of them eventually recorded songs they wrote or selected themselves, using producers and studios of their own choosing. But to some observers, Outlaw imagery was rooted almost as deeply in publicity as it was in substance.

Top left: Jerry Bradley and Waylon Jennings, c. 1975.

Left: Willie Nelson, 1967.
*Courtesy of Sony Music Archives*

Although Nelson and Jennings had larger profiles as so-called "outlaws," and RCA documents give Jennings sole producer credits for sessions as early as December 1972, Chet Atkins and Bobby Bare helped create a model for the artistic autonomy Jennings ultimately secured. After Bare left RCA in 1970 to record for Mercury for two years, Atkins enticed him back by suggesting that he produce himself—a practice then well established in rock but barely in its infancy in country music. In 1973 Bare released *Ride Me Down Easy* and *Bobby Bare Sings Lullabys, Legends and Lies*, albums that symbolized country's transition from record label staff producers who oversaw large artist rosters to independent producers, each of whom guided a small number of acts. Both collections were recorded in Studio B, where Bare had cut his 1960s hits.

Above: Kris Kristofferson, c. 1972.
*Courtesy of Sony Music Archives*

Above right: Waylon Jennings shares a laugh with Ronnie Milsap, mid-1970s.

Right: Ronnie Milsap's album *Pure Love* (RCA, 1974).

Even as outlaw hyperbole came and went, Bradley diversified RCA Nashville's roster by signing Ronnie Milsap, a champion of country-pop who recorded no less than sixty-two Top Ten country hits for the label, with thirty-five reaching #1. Most of these were cut at Studio A, Woodland, or Milsap's own studio, but some were made at Studio B. "I recorded half of my first RCA album at Studio B," the singer said. "That was *Where My Heart Is*. Lots of fans have told me they especially like my rendition of Kris Kristofferson's 'Please Don't Tell Me How the Story Ends,' which I cut in Studio B and included on my second RCA album, *Pure Love*."

Jerry Bradley kept upgrading Studio A and used it for almost all of the sessions he produced. Even so, Studio B remained active, with sessions by the RCA acts Johnny Russell, who had a #12 country hit with the story song "Catfish John" (1972 and 1973), and Gary Stewart, who topped the country charts in 1975 with his mournful "She's Actin' Single (I'm Drinkin' Doubles)." Using demos, work tapes, and overdubs, RCA singer-songwriter Guy Clark assembled his breakout 1975 album, *Old No. 1*, in Studio B. "L.A. Freeway," "Let Him Roll," and "Desperados Waiting for a Train" are some of its best-known tracks.

Other labels also used Studio B in the 1970s. Produced by her husband, Stan Silver, Donna Fargo recorded her self-penned "The Happiest Girl in the Whole U.S.A." for Dot in 1972. This release went #1 country and #11 pop; won a Grammy for Best Country Vocal Performance, Female; and was named BMI's most performed country song in 1973. Mickey Gilley, recording for the Playboy label, cut the #1 country hit "I Overlooked an Orchid" at the studio in 1974.

Top left: *Bobby Bare Sings Lullabys, Legends and Lies* (RCA, 1973).

Left: Donna Fargo's album *The Happiest Girl in the Whole USA* (Dot, 1972).

A tour at Historic RCA Studio B, 2016.

# Into the *Twenty-First Century*

In 1977, after longstanding disputes with the engineers' union, RCA Records closed most of its company studios nationwide. Owen and Jerry Bradley, in partnership with Harold Bradley and Chet Atkins, rebranded Studio A as Music City Music Hall, and moved most of Studio B's microphones there. Dan Maddox retained ownership of the Studio B *building*, and the Bradleys offered the rest of the equipment to the Country Music Hall of Fame and Museum. The museum began operating Studio B as a historic site that same year, after being encouraged by the Bradleys and Maddox to offer tours and school programs there. In 1992, the Maddox Family Foundation donated Studio B to the museum, and in the mid-1990s, the primary studio area was restored to its original look and a window was added through which visitors now can observe sessions. The Javelina recording enterprise leased Music City Music Hall for several years in the 1990s.

Connie Smith with an early portrait photo in the lobby of Historic RCA Studio B, 2010.
*Photo by Thomas Petrillo*

Fred Bogert, head of Studio C Productions, replaced Studio B's console and worked in Studio B from 1997 to 2000. During those years he facilitated a number of notable projects. Trout Fishing in America recorded the Grammy-nominated album *Infinity*. Award-winning fiddler Vassar Clements made his 1998 album *Back Porch Swing*, and the soundtrack for the David Carradine film *American Reel* was recorded during that time as well. David Amram, a world-renowned musician, composer, and conductor, recorded his critically acclaimed 1999 project *Southern Stories* in the historic space.

In 2002, the Mike Curb Family Foundation purchased RCA Studio B and leased it back to the museum in perpetuity for $1 a year. Museum staff members manage the studio, supervising school programs and public tours during the day. From 2001 to 2014, Belmont University's Mike Curb School of Music and Entertainment Business used Studio B to teach students historic and modern recording techniques. When the Belmont program stopped using the studio, the console was removed, and the museum eventually put in another console.

A number of artists have completed special projects at Studio B in the twenty-first century. For example, Americana artist Gillian Welch chose Studio B to record her 2001 album *Time (the Revelator)*. Martina McBride, Carrie Underwood, and LeAnn Rimes added parts to vintage Elvis Presley tracks for Presley's posthumously issued *Christmas Duets* (RCA, 2008).

Right: Images from Historic RCA Studio B, 2016.
*Photos by Bob Delevante*

Wynonna, Sara Evans, Amy Grant, Gretchen Wilson, Kimberly Schlapman and Karen Fairchild of Little Big Town, Anne Murray, and Olivia Newton-John also contributed to this project.

Marty Stuart released *Ghost Train: The Studio B Sessions* in 2010, and produced his wife, Connie Smith, when she recorded her 2011 Sugar Hill album *Long Line of Heartaches*. Both artists described their experiences especially for this book.

For his album *Darker than Light* (Plowboy, 2013), Bobby Bare returned to the place where he began his RCA years. "I recorded the album in Studio B because I was afraid it might get torn down," he said, "and I wanted to do one more album there before that happened. Fortunately, it didn't get torn down."

Considering its longevity, the many significant recordings made within its walls, and the diversity and excellence of the artists, producers, singers, musicians, and engineers who have created these cultural treasures, RCA Studio B stands as one of the most important studios in the history of sound recording. The Country Music Hall of Fame and Museum is proud to serve as guardian of Studio B's legacy, and to interpret this historic space for the schoolchildren, families, and adults who belong to the museum's ever-growing worldwide audience.

Top left: Elvis Presley, *Christmas Duets* (RCA, 2008).

Middle left: Gillian Welch, *Time (The Revelator)* (Acony, 2001)

Far left: Bobby Bare, *Darker than Light* (Plowboy, 2012)

Left: Bobby Bare in Studio B, 2013.
*Photo by Pete Mroz*
*Courtesy of Plowboy Records*

---

# "Ghost Train"

Connie Smith and Marty Stuart, 2010.
*Photo by Adam Smith*

Tradition-conscious Marty Stuart released *Ghost Train: The Studio B Sessions* on Sugar Hill Records in 2010. "I had the suspicion in my mind," Stuart said, "that if we were to restage sessions there, with the right songs and musicians, the studio would come to life as if it had never been asleep. We also wanted to raise public awareness of the studio—that it was a living, breathing, working studio, not just a museum piece. I took my band, the Fabulous Superlatives, and our engineer, to the studio. We walked it, talked it, and pondered it. We listened to hits that had been recorded there. At night, I kept thinking about the studio, and the ghost of the place and the legend of the place laid heavy on my mind, so I knew I made the right decision to record there. And we were really pleased with the results. One of the songs on *Ghost Train* was "Hummingbyrd," a tribute to Clarence White, which won a Grammy for Best Country Instrumental Performance. So we felt validated."

For one *Ghost Train* selection, Stuart called on his wife, Country Music Hall of Fame member Connie Smith, to sing with him on their original song "I Run to You." "When she came into the studio," Stuart said, "I knew that she was home. I remember her saying 'I've done so many sessions here that I automatically know where to point my voice to get the best sound.'"

Smith explained that her desire to meet Stuart's high standards sometimes put her on edge when working in his presence. But she felt much more relaxed when he used the studio to produce her 2011 Sugar Hill album *Long Line of Heartaches*. "We wrote so many of the songs together," she said, "and that let us get to know each other better."

Marty Stuart in the Studio B control room during the making of his 2010 album *Ghost Train*.
*Photo by Adam Smith*

# Recommended Listening

Two CDs compiled by the Country Music Hall of Fame® and Museum provide excellent examples of songs recorded in RCA Studio B: *Historic RCA Studio B Volume One* (Country Music Foundation Records, 2005) and *Historic RCA Studio B Volume Two* (Country Music Foundation Records, 1996, 2005). Both are available from the Country Music Hall of Fame and Museum. Visit www.CountryMusicHallofFame.org for details.

This list is a sampling of songs recorded at RCA Studio B. Some are included on the CDs mentioned above. Most were originally available on vinyl and are long out of print, though some can still be found in their original single and LP formats at local used record stores. Some have been reissued on CD or can be downloaded or streamed via digital online services such as iTunes, Pandora, Spotify, and YouTube. For more information on the artists and music listed here, visit www.StudioB.org.

### Eddy Arnold
"I Want to Go with You"
"Tennessee Stud"
"What's He Doing in My World"

### Chet Atkins
"Freight Train"
"Wheels"
"Yakety Axe"

### Bobby Bare
"Detroit City
"500 Miles Away from Home"
"Four Strong Winds"
"Shame on Me"

### Jim Ed Brown
"Pop a Top"

### The Browns
"The Old Lamplighter"
"Scarlet Ribbons (for Her Hair)"
"The Three Bells"

### Rosemary Clooney
"Anytime"
"Give Myself a Party"
"I Really Don't Want to Know"

### Perry Como
"My Own Peculiar Way"

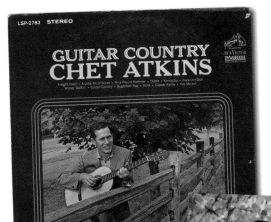

Chet Atkins,
*Guitar Country* (RCA, 1964).

Hank Locklin,
*Happy Journey* (RCA, 1962).

*Roger Miller* (RCA Camden, 1964).

**Floyd Cramer**
"Last Date"
"On the Rebound"
"San Antonio Rose"

**Skeeter Davis**
"Am I That Easy to Forget?"
"The End of the World"
"Silver Threads and Golden Needles"

**Duane Eddy**
"Country Twist"
"Crazy Arms"
"Fireball Mail"

**The Everly Brothers**
"All I Have to Do Is Dream"
"Cathy's Clown "
"So Sad (to Watch Good Love Go Bad)"

**Donna Fargo**
"The Happiest Girl in the Whole U.S.A"

**Don Gibson**
"I Can't Stop Lovin' You"
"(I'd Be) a Legend in My Time"
"Oh Lonesome Me"
"Sea of Heartbreak"

**Mickey Gilley**
"I Overlooked an Orchid"

**Bobby Goldsboro**
"Honey"

**Billy Grammer**
"Bonaparte's Retreat"
"Gotta Travel On"

**George Hamilton IV**
"Abilene"

**John Hartford**
"Gentle on My Mind"

**Al Hirt**
"Cotton Candy"
"Fancy Pants"
"Java"

**Waylon Jennings**
"Only Daddy That'll Walk the Line"
"Stop the World (and Let Me Off)"
"(That's What You Get) for Lovin' Me"

**Grandpa Jones**
"T for Texas"

**Hank Locklin**
"Followed Closely by My Teardrops"
"Happy Birthday to Me"
"Please Help Me, I'm Falling"

**Bob Luman**
"Let's Think About Living"

**Rose Maddox**
"Roll in My Sweet Baby's Arms"

**Roger Miller**
"Lock, Stock and Teardrops"
"When Two Worlds Collide"
"You Don't Want My Love"

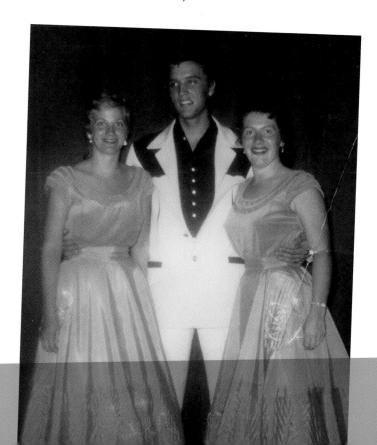

Elvis and the Davis Sisters, c. 1956.
Left to right: Skeeter Davis, Elvis Presley,
Georgia Davis.

# *Recommended Listening* (continued)

**Ronnie Milsap**
"I Hate You"
"Please Don't Tell Me How the Story Ends"
"That Girl Who Waits on Tables"

**Roy Orbison**
"Crying"
"In Dreams"
"Only the Lonely"

**Dolly Parton**
"Coat of Many Colors"
"I Will Always Love You"
"Joshua"

**Elvis Presley**
"Are You Lonesome Tonight?"
"How Great Thou Art"
"It's Now or Never"
"Little Sister"

**Charley Pride**
"Is Anybody Goin' to San Antone"
"Just Between You and Me"
"Kiss an Angel Good Mornin'"

**Boots Randolph**
"Yakety Sax"

**Jim Reeves**
"He'll Have to Go"
"I Know One"
"Welcome to My World"

**Jim Reeves and Dottie West**
"Love Is No Excuse"

**Charlie Rich**
"Big Boss Man"
"There Won't Be Anymore"

**Connie Smith**
"Nobody But a Fool (Would Love You)"
"Once a Day"
"The Hurtin's All Over"

**Hank Snow**
"Breakfast with the Blues"
"I've Been Everywhere"
"Miller's Cave"

**Gary Stewart**
"She's Actin' Single (I'm Drinkin' Doubles)"
"Out of Hand"

**Marty Stuart**
"Branded"
"Country Boy Rock & Roll"
"Hummingbyrd"

**Porter Wagoner**
"Green, Green Grass of Home"
"I've Enjoyed as Much of This as I Can Stand"
"Misery Loves Company"

**Gillian Welch**
"Dear Someone"
"I Want to Sing That Rock & Roll"
"Revelator"

**Dottie West**
"Here Comes My Baby"
"Would You Hold It Against Me"

Top: *Best of Dolly Parton* (RCA, 1975).

Bottom: Waylon Jennings, *Only the Greatest* (RCA, 1968).

# Sources

## BOOKS

Atkins, Chet, and Michael Cochran. *Chet Atkins—Me and My Guitars.* West Plains, Missouri: Russ Cochran, 2001; New York: Hal Leonard, 2003.

Atkins, Chet, with Bill Neely. *Country Gentleman.* Chicago: H. Regnery, 1974.

Davis, Skeeter. *Bus Fare to Kentucky: The Autobiography of Skeeter Davis.* New York: Carol Publishing Group, 1993.

Emery, Ralph, with Tom Carter. *More Memories.* New York: G. P. Putnam's Sons, 1993.

Eng, Steve. *A Satisfied Mind: The Country Music Life of Porter Wagoner.* Nashville: Rutledge Hill Press, 1992.

Guralnick, Peter. *Last Train to Memphis: The Rise of Elvis Presley.* Boston: Little, Brown, and Co., 1994.

————. *Careless Love: The Unmaking of Elvis Presley.* Boston: Little, Brown, and Co., 1999.

Hawkins, Martin. *A Shot in the Dark: Making Records in Nashville, 1945–1955.* Nashville: Vanderbilt University Press and the Country Music Foundation Press, 2006.

Jorgensen, Ernst. *Elvis Presley, A Life in Music: The Complete Recording Sessions.* New York: St. Martin's Press, 1998.

Kingsbury, Paul, and Alanna Nash, eds. *Will the Circle Be Unbroken: Country Music in America.* Foreword by Willie Nelson. New York: DK Publishing, 2006.

Malone, Bill C., and Judith McCulloh, eds., *Stars of Country Music: Uncle Dave Macon to Johnny Rodriguez.* Urbana: Univ. of Illinois Press, 1975. See William Ivey, "Chet Atkins," 274–88.

Nelson, Willie, with Bud Shrake. *Willie: An Autobiography.* New York: Simon and Schuster, 1988.

Pride, Charley, with Jim Henderson. *Pride: The Charley Pride Story.* New York: William Morrow, 1994.

Sanjek, Russell. *From Print to Plastic: Publishing and Promoting America's Popular Music (1900–1980).* Brooklyn: Institute for Studies in American Music, 1983.

## ARTICLES

Atkins, Chet. "Chet Atkins, Part I." *Guitar Player,* February 1972, 20–25, 39.

————. "Chet Atkins, Part II." *Guitar Player,* March 1972, 30–33.

McVey, Richard II. "Studio B." *Music City News,* June 1996, 54, 58, 12.

Rumble, John W. "The Emergence of Nashville as a Recording Center: Logbooks from the Castle Studio, 1952–1953." *Journal of Country Music* 7, no. 3 (December 1978): 22–41.

1967 Ampeq Amp.
*Photo by Bob Delevante*

# Sources (continued)

## BUSINESS DOCUMENTS

All available at the Frist Library and Archives,
Country Music Hall of Fame and Museum, Nashville, Tenn.

American Federation of Musicians, Local 257, session contracts.

RCA Records session files.

Art Satherley and Don Law Columbia Records Notebooks.

## INTERNET

Praguefrank.com is helpful for researching recording session data,
taken largely from record company files.

## INTERVIEWS

*All interviews conducted by the author unless otherwise noted.*

Arnold, Eddy: Sept. 12, 2000; July 1, 2002.

Atkins, Chet: Sept. 18, 1992.

Atkins, Chet, and Owen Bradley, interviewed by Lewis Anderson:
July 2, 1992.

Babcock, Joe: Dec. 15, 2015.

Bare, Bobby: April 20, 2001; Dec. 17, 2015.

Bradley, Harold: Sept. 15, 1988; April 12, 2011.

Bradley, Jerry: April 27, 2012; Dec. 1, 2015.

Brown, Jim Ed: April 21, 2011.

Clement, Jack, interviewed by John Lomax III: May 13, 1978.

Davis, Danny, and Bill Collins: Nov. 28, 1995.

Edenton, Ray: April 9, 2011; Jan. 15, 2016.

Foglesong, Jim: June 5, 1992.

Foster, Fred: Nov. 15, 2000; Nov. 29, 2000; Jan.15, 2016.

1974 Hammond B3 organ. *Photo by Bob Delevante*

Galante, Joe: April 17, 1986.

Hamilton, George IV: May 3, 2011.

Harris, Bill: Dec. 13, 2015.

Harris, Ina, and Bill Vandervort, interviewed by Karolyn Freeman: Dec. 4, 1980.

Light, Ronny: Jan. 9, 2016.

Loudermilk, John D.: April 19, 2011.

McCuen, Brad, interviewed by Douglas B. Green: April 29, 1975.

Milsap, Ronnie: Dec. 17, 2015.

Moore, Bob: April 15, 2001.

Nunley, Louis: April 12, 2001.

Ron Oates: Dec. 1, 2015.

Parton, Dolly, interviewed by Peter Greenberg: Oct. 5, 2015.

Porter, Bill: Feb. 23, 1994; June 8, 1994; Nov. 13, 1994.

Snoddy, Glen: Aug. 9, 1983; Aug. 15, 1983.

Wariner, Steve: Jan. 6, 2016.

# Acknowledgments

Many persons assisted in the preparation of this book, including recording artists, executives, producers, studio musicians and vocalists, and engineers. The Country Music Hall of Fame and Museum appreciates the contributions of each of these individuals, including those who were interviewed—many of whom provided photos and helped to identify them. (Please see list of persons interviewed in the Sources section.)

In addition, we are grateful to the museum's senior digital content manager Michael Manning, who provided many album covers from his extensive collection of recordings, as well as Professor Michael Janas of the Mike Curb School of Music Business and Entertainment, independent researcher Brenda Colladay, and Twyla Lambert Clark, of Nashville's Lithographics, Inc.

Since the early 1960s, ambient lighting has played an important role in Studio B sessions. Elvis Presley, for instance, had the lights turned off completely when he recorded "Are You Lonesome Tonight?" in 1960. Engineer Bill Porter brought in Christmas lights and decorations to set the mood for a Chet Atkins Christmas album. At left are three basic lighting schemes that can be blended for various effects.

*Photos by Bob Delevante*

Historic RCA Studio B, 2016
*Photo by Ron Coons*

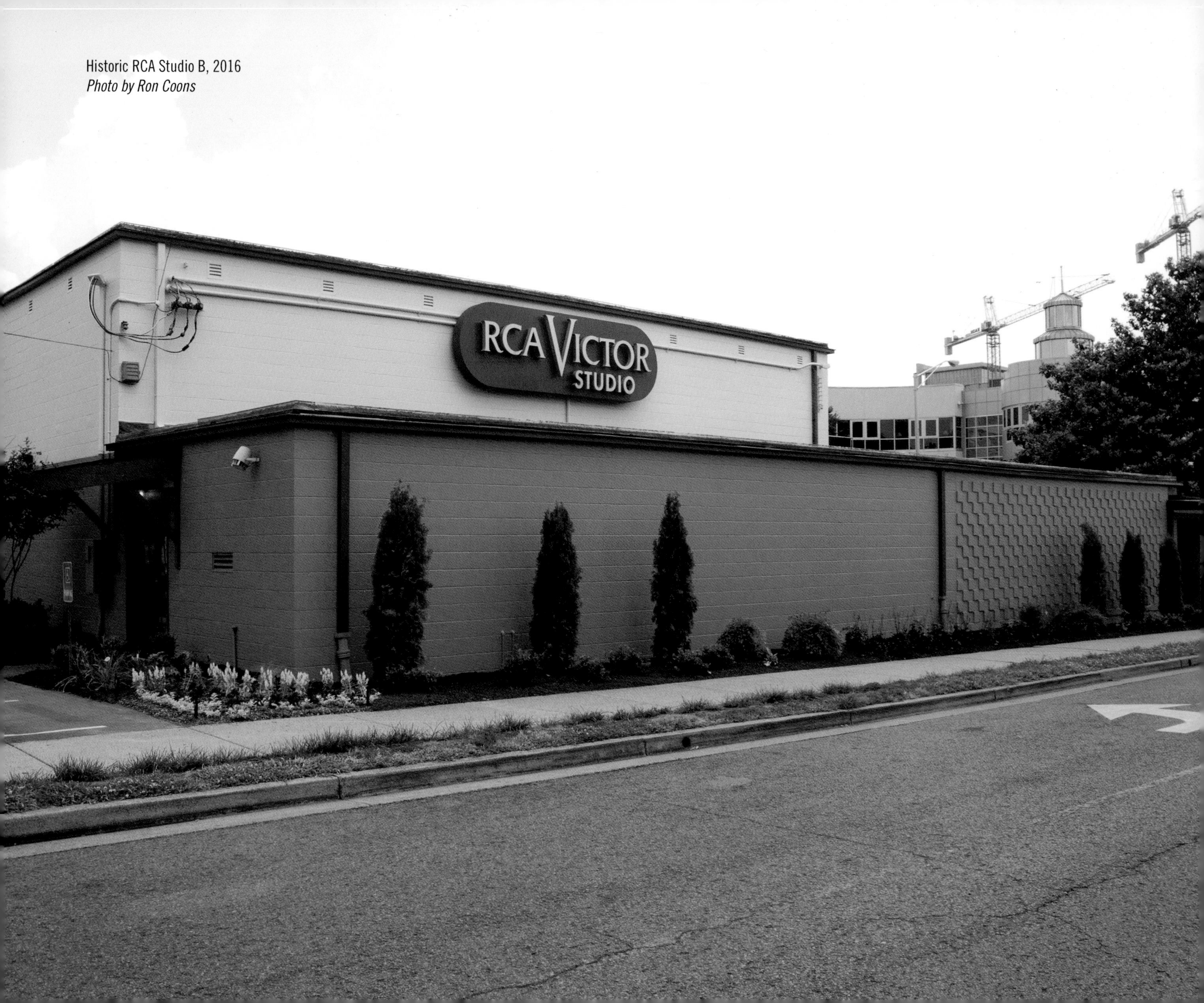